# First Lady

## A Portrait of
## Nancy Reagan

From the NBC White Paper
reported by White House
Correspondent Chris Wallace

St. Martin's Press
New York

FIRST LADY. Copyright ©1986 by National Broadcasting Corporation, Inc.
All rights reserved. Printed in the United States of America.
No part of this book may be used or reproduced in any manner whatsoever without written permission except in the case of brief quotations embodied in critical articles or reviews. For information, address St. Martin's Press, 175 Fifth Avenue, New York, N.Y. 10010.

Library of Congress Cataloging in Publication Data
National Broadcasting Corporation, Inc.
    First lady.

    1. Reagan, Nancy, 1923–. 2. Reagan, Ronald.
3. Presidents—United States—Wives—Biography.
I. Title.
E878.R43W35  1986      973.927'092'4  [B]  86-14255
ISBN 0-312-29243-0

Design by Laura Hough
First Edition
10 9 8 7 6 5 4 3 2 1

# Contents

# Acknowledgments

A great many people helped create the "First Lady" documentary and this book. Among those most intimately involved at NBC were: Percy Arrington, Susan Beckett, Dwight Brown, Jim Burt, D. M. Therese Byrn, Bob Caminiti, Thomas Dawson, Judy Ellen Doctoroff, Charles Fekete, Constantine S. Gochis, Al Hoaglund, Natalie Hunter, John Lane, Paula Banks Mashore, Robert McFarland, David McGloin, Kim Mogul, Tom Pettit, Robert Rogers, Charles Russell, Daine Forman Russell, Bruce Schachat, Rhonda Schwartz, Al Storey, Michael Tcherkassky, James White, Tom Wolzien. Michael Kilian was enormously helpful in editing several thousand pages of transcripts. At St. Martin's Press, Andy Carpenter, Margaret Schwarzer, Jill Grafflin, Elizabeth Williams, and Amit Shah put in extra hours in the design, layout, and manufacturing of the book. Special thanks are also in order to the First Lady's press secretary, Elaine Crispen, and her assistant, Mary Gordon, who were most helpful in the selection of the photography. They were invariably courteous and gracious despite a very busy schedule.

# *Introduction*

*I*t was a White House correspondent's nightmare come true. The President of the United States was standing three feet up the hill, beckoning me to come with him. Normally that would be a rare opportunity, not a problem. But a problem it was, because at that moment the First Lady of the United States was standing three feet down the hill, asking me to join her. It was a moment worthy of Talleyrand—and I hope I did not shame him. Addressing the First Couple of the United States, standing uneasily between them, I said, "If you think I'm going to choose, you're crazy. You two work it out."

The occasion was a fine spring day in April 1985 at Rancho del Cielo, the Reagan ranch in the Santa Ynez mountains of California. I was there along with a producer, two camera crews, a light man, and a unit manager shooting an NBC News documentary on Mrs. Reagan. It was supposed to be an opportunity to see the First Lady in an informal setting—what her life was like away from the White House, the designer dresses, and the fancy receptions. But I had gotten more informality than I bargained for. And in the four months I spent with Nancy Reagan, for the documentary—it was one of the several key incidents that told me a lot about her.

We had a good day at the ranch, shooting pictures of the First Couple riding, her serving him lunch ("Just like usual," he said to her with a wink), and driving in a pickup truck.

Now it was time to do an extensive interview with Mrs. Reagan on her personal life. While she ducked into the ranch house to get ready, the President started talking about an outhouse he had put on the hill next to his home to store his tools.

"Come see it," he said, and we headed up the hill, just as Mrs. Reagan walked out of the house and asked where we were going.

"I want to take Chris up to the outhouse," the President said.

"But the camera crew is ready. You're holding up everything." Mrs. Reagan replied, the worshipful gaze she focuses on her husband in public nowhere to be seen.

That was when I bowed out, wanting no part of this First Family Feud. But Mr. Reagan stood tall, "It will only take a moment."

"But everything's ready," Mrs. Reagan said with some exasperation. And then, "All right, but don't spend too long there."

It may not be Eugene O'Neill, but there was a clear subtext to this family spat: Ronnie, I've spent twenty years standing in the background, having TV crews push me out of the way to cover you. Now, for once, a reporter is here to talk to me. The cameras are here to take my picture. Please, darling, don't muck it up.

The idea for a documentary on Nancy Reagan came out of a dinner I had in January 1985 with NBC News president Larry Grossman. We started talking about how Mrs. Reagan had grown in the job—from a very rough start when she was severely criticized for spending too much time on clothes and china—to a point where she was widely praised for her campaign against drug abuse. Her husband had just won forty-nine states in his reelection effort, but some polls showed that the Reagan with the highest approval rating was named Nancy.

It seemed to us that there was an interesting story here—or rather, several interesting stories: how Nancy Reagan had turned around her image; whether there was a real change in the woman or just clever public relations; whether she was actually the behind-the-scenes influence on policy that had long been rumored; how to understand this loving wife who had such stormy relations with her children.

NBC News spent the next four months covering those stories. We took our cameras to places the Reagans had never before allowed them: a weekend at Camp David; sending the President off from the White House family quarters to make a major speech. We accompanied Mrs. Reagan to the Vatican where she discussed her anti-drug campaign with Pope John Paul. Most important, we talked to the people who know Mrs. Reagan best—her family (except for her daughter Patti, who refused), her friends, and to top Reagan staffers. By far the greatest insights, though, came in several extensive conversations with Nancy Reagan herself, in which she talked openly and more frankly than she ever had before about her personal life, her political clout, and her growing willingness to "go public" about her role. We ended up with the first prime-time documentary on a First Lady—not a tour of the White House, but a serious examination of her role and views.

This book is the fruit of those interviews: not a formal biography, but rather an oral history of Mrs. Reagan taken from twenty-eight perspectives, a portrait of the First Lady by the people who know her best. Right here, I want to recognize the work of executive producer Robert Rogers and producers Paula Mashore and Rhonda Schwartz. They did several of the interviews and came up with most of the ideas.

As a political reporter, what interested me most in this project was how to find out if Mrs. Reagan was as powerful as people said she was. The answer was: even more powerful.

I had heard that she regularly called a few top Presidential aides to discuss policies or her husband's schedule. But as I talked to people in the White House, I discovered that the network was much wider and far more important. I learned that Mrs. Reagan called the personnel office to suggest appointments, that she spoke to campaign officials to discuss the nuts and bolts of the reelection effort. Most important, top aides told me—and Mrs. Reagan later confirmed—she played a key role during the 1984 campaign in turning around the President's policy toward the Soviets—ending the hard-line rhetoric and sending out feelers for negotiations—that in no small part blunted Democratic charges that Mr. Reagan might get the country into a war. The First Lady generally sided with moderates over hard-line conservatives, being more interested in seeing her husband win than in ideology.

I also found that most people around Mrs. Reagan were afraid of her. I reduced one top official to stuttering simply by asking, "Are you a little scared of her?" The people who felt confident of their relationship with her were the most honest. Campaign strategist Stuart Spencer talked about what a tough enemy she could be—that after he backed Gerald Ford against Reagan in 1976, she treated him as a "leper," refusing to talk to him for years. Son Ron said, "She can be a handful. I mean, she's not always the easiest person to get along with.... I don't think I'd want her to be my boss."

In talking to people about the First Lady, one word kept coming up again and again: When she wants something, Nancy Reagan is "relentless." I was to learn that firsthand. During the work on our documentary, Mrs. Reagan was a total pro. She gave us surprising access to her daily life and never applied any pressure on what we could say. But there was one exception: She wanted Frank Sinatra on the program.

We had been following her for several weeks when Mrs. Reagan suddenly asked if I was going to interview Sinatra. I was a little surprised—I didn't think of Sinatra as a close friend of hers, and I wouldn't have thought she would suggest him, with his alleged link to the Mob, as a character witness. But she said that they had talked, and he was willing to do it. Every few weeks after that she would call—or have an aide call—to ask how we were doing with Sinatra. The conclusion I came to was that Mrs. Reagan had never quite gotten over her girlhood crush on Sinatra, and if a documentary was being done on her life, she wanted Frank in it.

The problem was that President Reagan and Pope John Paul were far more cooperative than Sinatra was. We talked to lawyers, agents, and secretaries and each had a demand: there could be no editing of Mr. Sinatra's interview; we had to submit the questions in advance to Mr. Sinatra; Mr. Sinatra would consent to an interview in his Las Vegas dressing room on a certain night. And, as I said, every few weeks I'd get a call from Mrs. Reagan or an assistant asking how the interview was coming along.

By this point, we had shot the rest of the documentary and decided to tell Mr. Sinatra thanks, but no thanks. But I then had the unpleasant duty of informing Mrs. Reagan. It is remarkable how quiet the other end of a phone line can get.

But before you try to pigeonhole Mrs. Reagan, let me confuse you. The First Lady is one of the most vulnerable, warmest, funniest people I have ever met. Doug Wick, the son of close Reagan friend Charles Wick, described her as "one of the greatest lunch dates in America." I know what he meant.

We went with Mrs. Reagan to Arizona one day to see her ailing, eighty-eight-year-old mother. I was riding on an Air Force DC-9 with her, and we ended up spending the entire four-hour flight chatting together. There are not many members of your own family with whom you would want to spend that length of time. With Mrs. Reagan, it was easy.

First of all, unlike most public figures, she does not talk just about herself. She asks what's on your mind, and, even more unusual, remembers your answers. She's interested in everything—Washington gossip, the latest movies, how your kids are doing. And she has a remarkable ability to fasten her big, doe like eyes on you—and make you feel very important.

Mrs. Reagan also projects a vulnerability that is appealing and genuine. She may be a woman who has talked with emperors and dined in palaces, but there is still a lot of little Nancy Davis in her. Mrs. Reagan did not have a storybook childhood. Her father left the family when she was a baby, and her mother—who was an actress—left soon after. Nancy was brought up by an aunt and uncle. She remembers visiting her father once and, after they got into an argument about her mother, being locked in the bathroom. Finally, when Nancy was seven, her mother married a wealthy Chicago surgeon, Loyal Davis, and reclaimed her.

Perhaps as a result, there is a sense of frailty just beneath Mrs. Reagan's glittery surface. During a long interview at the California ranch, she began to cry as she talked about the death of Dr. Davis in 1982 and about how much she missed him.

But possibly even more poignant were her comments about relations between mothers and children. Mrs. Reagan calls her mother everyday, no matter what she is doing or where in the world she is. "It's always been difficult for me to understand how children could turn against their mothers or be separated from their mothers," she said. "For all those others who had their mothers, I wanted to say to them, 'You're so lucky... you've had all those wonderful years that I never had.'"

It is one of those strange contradictions in life that Mrs. Reagan has often had strained relations with her own children. Son Ron had an explanation, saying Mrs. Reagan's childhood has "given her the desire for a close family and a family structure that's idealized in a certain way and one that no family can really live up to."

The most interesting development we found during the time we spent with Mrs. Reagan, however, was that after years of playing "wife of . . ." she was finally ready to step forward and let people understand her true role in the Reagan phenomenon. I can't overstate what a big change this was for her.

I had interviewed Mrs. Reagan in March of 1981, shortly after she became First Lady. She was the ultimate politician's wife saying the kinds of things that had long set feminists' teeth to gnashing. Her life "began," she said, when she "met Ronnie." How would she balance her role as wife with her new responsibilities as First Lady? No question, she said, the role of wife, of making Ronnie comfortable, would always come first—and, in fact, was the most important part of being First Lady.

The woman I interviewed in 1985 still did not meet Betty Friedan's standards—but she had a very different sense of herself. She was proud of what she had accomplished in her campaign against drug abuse. And, for the first time, she wanted people to know she was a key part of her husband's success.

Mrs. Reagan's interest in drug abuse is revealing because I believe it started out largely as a public relations effort. Mrs. Reagan had long had a vague interest in the drug issue, along with the Foster Grandparents program and other good works. But in late 1981, when the "Queen Nancy" controversy was reaching its height, Presidential pollster Richard Wirthlin and Reagan strategist Michael Deaver decided to try to dispel that image with a big push against drugs.

The First Lady was soon touring the country, hugging kids who had beaten drug addiction, and urging parents to get involved. And in the course of this campaign, several interesting things happened. First, Mrs. Reagan saw that she could have an impact. Mike Deaver told me she realized "that she is in a position for the first time in her life to be more than just Mrs. Ronald Reagan, that she can do something with her life independently that can make a change for the good."

In addition, the anti-drug effort was a big success—and part of Mrs. Reagan seemed to blossom with the applause. During the making of the documentary, I asked the First Lady if she had become more self-confident. "Yes," she said, "because I think, maybe, more people like me. And if I think people like me, I'm better."

There was a dramatic illustration of that when Mrs. Reagan went to the Vatican to discuss her anti-drug campaign with Pope John Paul. She had met the Pope before, but always as the wife of the President. This time she was meeting him in her own right to talk about her own project. Her aides pointed out that she wore a business suit—instead of a long dress and veil—because she was there on business. And after her Papal audience, she was glowing with excitement. "It was," she said, "one of the most moving, wonderful experiences I've ever had. I've met him twice before, but this was the first time alone." By *alone*, what she meant was: without her husband.

I don't mean to overstate here, because Mrs. Reagan is still a traditional wife—devoted to her husband, fiercely protective of his interests, and clearly willing to take a supporting role. It's just that she now realizes there's plenty of spotlight left for her.

Whenever Mrs. Reagan had been asked before about her White House clout, her answer, in effect, was "Who me?" But after I had gotten a number of top advisers to talk—on camera—about what an important player she was, I decided to try to get her to come clean.

Just before a long interview in the White House family quarters, I took Mrs. Reagan aside. "We have all these people calling you a tough, savvy politician," I said. "If you get on TV and giggle, you're going to look a little silly." But I don't think the pep talk was necessary, because it was soon evident that the First Lady had come to the same conclusion.

"I think I'm aware of people who are trying to take advantage of my husband," she said. "All of my little antennas go up." What happened when she saw that? "I try to stop it."

Mrs. Reagan then told me how she wanted to cut the deadwood out of the Cabinet after the 1984 election. (She doesn't win them all. The President asked the entire Cabinet to stay on.) As I said earlier, she acknowledged playing a key role in the turnaround in Administration policy toward preparations for Mr. Reagan's first debate with Walter Mondale, in which he gave a fumbling performance. Were any changes made? "Well," she said with a broad smile, "the second debate was better, wasn't it?"

Mrs. Reagan will never satisfy the feminists, but, in a sense, she has been liberated during her years in the White House—liberated by her new popularity and the confidence that has generated, liberated by her greater awareness of the platform she enjoys, liberated by the simple fact that she'll never have to face another election.

And so, as the Reagan years play out, we will have to assess not only the President's place in history, but also Mrs. Reagan's. What will her place be? My guess is that she won't be loved—or hated—as Eleanor Roosevelt was. Her public persona is too reserved, too dispassionate for that. She won't be idolized as Jacqueline Kennedy was. We're no longer that innocent. My guess is that she will be respected—as a very good wife working hard at the many aspects of a demanding job. And, as the years pass, my guess is that we will be surprised to learn how much influence she had on key decisions.

During one of our conversations I asked Mrs. Reagan whether she felt she had grown in her time as First Lady. "I don't know how you could help but grow," she said. "I mean, in a way, even the negative things that all happened in the beginning were probably part of a growth process."

And then we had this exchange:

*Question*: How do you explain the fact that people seem to like and be impressed with Nancy Reagan now?

*Answer*: I hope they like me. But I think it's been a process of getting to know me. And that took a long time.

It did take a long time—for all of us—and for Mrs. Reagan herself.

*Nancy and her mother in January 1931.*

# 1

# *Before the White House*

## NANCY REAGAN

*W*hen I was four, my mother left me in Bethesda, Maryland, and went off touring. She had to. She had to earn a living and she couldn't take me touring all over the country with her. When she would get a play that ran for a while in New York, then I'd go to New York and be with her. But the times in Bethesda with my aunt and uncle and my cousin Charlotte were very happy times. I have pictures of us on the Fourth of July with Ginger, our wirehaired terrier, and a bike all decorated for the Fourth. Charlotte and I put Fourth of July costumes on, and it was happy—except that I missed my mother.

It was a real ache. My aunt and uncle were nice, but your mother is your mother, and nobody can fill that spot. It was hard on me and it was hard on her.

I went to New York once on one of those occasions when I could visit and stay with her. She was in a play. I've forgotten what it was. But it was a play in which they were very mean to her—oh, they were awful to her. And I got so upset that, sitting up there in a box, watching, I began to cry. I guess I created quite a commotion. Then, when I went backstage, I wouldn't talk to anybody because they'd been mean to my mother. And Mother had to finally take me aside

and say, "Nancy, it's just make-believe. They're really nice. That was all just make-believe. They don't really feel that way about me."

Another time I visited my real father and he locked me in a bathroom. I'm sure that afterwards he felt badly about, well, lots of things that had happened. I was always reluctant to talk about it when he was alive because there was no point in hurting him. But this was a visit, and I remember something had been said about my mother that I didn't like. We got into an argument and I was locked in the bathroom. Ever since then I can't stand a locked door.

My stepmother, his wife, was a nice woman, and she came and got me out. But when we were first married, I remember my husband was going to lock a door and I wouldn't let him—he never knew this story. I said, "No, please, I don't want the door locked." And he couldn't understand why, and then I told him the story.

It wasn't all marvelous for a little girl. But there were nice times, too. My aunt and uncle were darling people, and so was my cousin. But I didn't have my mother.

When finally we were together, maybe I appreciated it more than if that hadn't happened to me. And it's always been difficult for me to understand how children could turn against their mother or be separated from their mother voluntarily. I never could understand that, particularly during the sixties when all the turmoil and so on between parents and children began. I had a hard time understanding that. For all those others who had their mothers, I wanted to say to them, "You're so lucky, you're just so lucky, you've had all those wonderful years that I never had."

When my mother met Loyal Davis and brought me to Chicago, it was like the happy ending to a fairy tale. She came to Bethesda to tell me that she'd met this wonderful man and she wanted to marry him, but she wouldn't marry him unless it was all right with me. And I often think, What in the world would have happened if I had said no? I think she would have gotten around it somehow, but I said yes, of course, and we went to Chicago. And I really couldn't have asked for a more wonderful father. He was a hard act to follow, but I think, with my husband, I followed it pretty well.

I graduated from college at a time when a lot of Smith graduates were getting married. I had people say to me afterwards, "You know, the rest of us stayed back there in Chicago and got married and had children and settled down. And you didn't—you went off to New York and Hollywood and to making movies and doing plays."

I hadn't found a man I wanted to marry. And I couldn't sit in Chicago and do nothing. I stayed with Mother until my

*For all those others who had their mothers, I wanted to say to them, "You're so lucky, you're just so lucky, you've had all those wonderful years that I never had."*

Right: *Nancy and her stepbrother, Dick (Dr. Richard Davis), in 1934.*

Below: *Nancy Davis and Ronald Reagan in* Hellcats of the Navy, *1957*

father went overseas, and I stayed for almost a year. And then, when he came back, I left Chicago. I hadn't found the right guy. So you do something, and acting was the only thing I knew. I mean, I'd been raised around it. Whatever you do, you want to do it as well as you can and accomplish as much as you can. That was inside me.

I liked acting. Not enough to keep on after I was married, but I liked it. It was fun and I met some great people. I met my husband that way.

I think I was pretty good. The first movie that really kicked it off was *The Next Voice You Hear.* I was sent to New York for a promotion tour. I remember going to Radio City and taking a picture of the marquee with my name up on it, and, oh, I was impressed. But I think my favorite picture was one with Ray Milland and Johnny Hodiak, *Night Into Morning.* I liked that picture the best.

There wasn't any big decision I had to make after I knew I was going to be married. For me, the real fulfillment came with marriage, a home, and children of my own. That was completing the whole thing for me. And I had the best of two worlds. I'd had a career that I was happy in and fairly successful in, and I had the marriage. I can't say to somebody else, "You should do it my way." I know what made me happy, and when I say, my life began then, that's what I thought. Maybe that's not true for somebody else, but it was for me.

*I hadn't found the right guy. So you do something, and acting was the only thing I knew.*

## DR. RICHARD DAVIS

*O*ur childhood together dates back to the thirties and forties, when we were growing up in Chicago. We were particularly blessed with two splendid parents who were devoted to one another and to us. We had a very stable home and the opportunity for an education. And we had some wonderful young friends.

My first memory of Nancy was probably when she was in the third or fourth grade. In those days, she wore a school uniform: tunic, knee socks, and a beret. At the beginning of the school year, my father and I would walk her to the corner of the drive and get her off to school. She had a bouncy gait, was very vivacious, and was a happy child. She would speak to everyone on the way. With each step, this tunic, which was too short, would sort of pop up in the air and we'd see her bloomers. Father would say, "Richard, Nancy has on those dreadful midnight blue bloomers, doesn't she?" And I would dutifully agree. And then he'd say, with a big, broad smile, "Isn't she just the most wonderful child?"

We played some outrageous games. We had one called "Help, Murder, Police!" This was a very precarious game. We'd both get on the highest piece of furniture and then jump on a sliding stool. And this went on and was very

*We were particularly blessed with two splendid parents who were devoted to one another and to us.*

Left: *Nancy, her mother, and Dr. Loyal Davis, June 1931.*

carefully timed for Dad's return home. By that time, we were totally exhausted, feigned broken arms and legs, and, of course, the great surgeon had to heal us. Then we went on with the evening's activities.

I have some of the most pleasant memories of the summers. We spent two summers with Mother and Dad as guests of Walter Huston and his wife in the San Bernadino Mountains. The days were filled with a lot of outdoor activity—hiking, riding, swimming, tennis. Of course, those were pre-television days, so we all entertained one another at night. Each of us read aloud from a novel during the six weeks—or sometimes poetry, Shakespeare. My father invariably put us all to sleep, and then Walter Huston would say, "Well, that's all right, Loyal. I hope you're a better neurosurgeon than an actor." There were many, many happy times during those summers.

One summer, we wrote, directed, and actually photographed our own little play. Nancy played opposite the great Walter Huston. She had a bathing suit on and was wrapped in a very elaborate sheet. At one point, he said, "Nancy, you're doing this far too demurely. Be more wicked and evil." And Nancy looked at me. I was photographing all this with a home movie camera. Neither one of us knew what demure meant. We found out later on. But I think if she ever made what we call today a career decision about drama and the theater, it was probably back in those really very terribly happy days in the thirties.

She really adored Dr. Loyal, her new father, so to speak. There was a great relationship between the two of them even when she was small, which she carried on all through her adult life. They were extremely close. The family, the whole concept of the family, and the camaraderie, the laughter, the enjoyment of one another, has been extremely important to her—as a youngster and throughout her adult life.

Dad was an extraordinarily devoted person, to his wife and to both of us. He was a rock-hard disciplinarian. When he asked either one of us to do something, we always did it to the best of our ability and we did it promptly. He was extremely fair. He was never unreasonable. But he thought basically that children with privilege should have responsibility. And we were reminded, not constantly, but often enough, that we had the responsibility to be excellent and to strive, to meet the challenges, in anything we did.

He was the key figure in Nancy's life. There's no question about that. She was very open with Dad. The day's activities centered around the dinner table. Some of the topics that Nancy brought up as a youngster and as a teenager were really quite extraordinary. It wasn't that infrequently that we discussed the soul. She asked him one

*She really adored Dr. Loyal. There was a great relationship between the two of them even when she was small, which she carried on all through her adult life.*

*Young Nancy and her stepfather, approximately 1929.*

night, I remember, what he thought happiness was. He said, "Nancy, the answer to happiness is almost twenty-five hundred years old and it's basically what the Greeks said. It's the pursuit of excellence in all aspects of one's life." That's a very serious and heavy answer, and I'm sure in hindsight Nancy and I would have a few things to add to that today. But she was always very open with him. She sought his advice, and once she got it, she followed it. She was extremely respectful and courteous, and extremely pleasant, not only with her peers but with older people.

We were disciplined. A principle was expounded and then the reasons for following that principle were explained. Dad never raised his voice with Nancy. He did with me occasionally.

We were very close, particularly in the summertime. Our educations were rather staggered. Sometimes I was home and she was away, but we were always together at Christmas and holidays.

Nancy was not at all politically minded. I think she became politically aware when she met the President in the early fifties in California. We discussed all sorts of political issues at home, but I don't think Nancy was that deeply concerned about politics. Her love was the theater.

I think there's an element of truth in the talk that Dad was a sounding board at the time the President was turning from Democrat to Republican. He was a good listener and he also gave the two of them advice. Perhaps he helped move the President off center in the sixties when he decided to enter politics. I think ultimately Dad was a really pivotal person in the whole mechanism of decision making. She probably followed the same line of thinking that her father did, which was not really along liberal lines.

One night, during a Christmas vacation, she came home from college and said, "Dad, I really have a heavy problem for the holidays. I have to learn all these sonnets by Keats and Shelley." Dad looked at her. The problem was attacked directly, met head on. She was sent upstairs for her English literature book and brought it downstairs, and the four of us learned parts of these sonnets. He was very pleased with this pursuit of excellence. I turned around and there was Edith, an actress, of course, and she had gotten up from the dinner table and was doing a little soft-shoe number and dancing and had thought up a little rhyme about Mr. Sheets and Mr. Kelly. This was the lighthearted side of our home life, and it was a good counterbalance between a very serious and intent father and a mother who had a really wonderful sense of humor.

# 2

# *The Real Nancy*

## NANCY REAGAN

*I*'m not going to be like anybody else. I'm going to be Nancy Reagan. I don't think I'm any different than I've always been. But anybody who doesn't grow in this position has got to be pretty dumb. I certainly hope I've grown. I think I have. I don't know how you could help but grow. You're exposed to so many different things, so many different people, so many different experiences. In a way, even the negative things that all happened in the beginning were probably part of a growth process. It widens your whole life, your horizons.

I'm more self-confident, I think, because, maybe, more people like me. If I think people like me, I'm better.

## WILLIAM F. BUCKLEY

*T*here's a difference between self-confidence and being assertive. I think that Nancy Reagan has always intentionally cultivated two roles—one public and the other private. In private surroundings, she will let her opinion be known. In public situations, she is deferential, not in the sense that she feels women should be subordinate

in public circumstances, but because she feels that it's her husband who has been elected. There are two personalities there.

She's a wonderful friend. She will really struggle to do you a kindness or help you in anything that you want. I make it a point not to ask powerful people for favors, but if I thought that without upsetting public policy she could be helpful, I would simply ask her. I don't doubt for a moment that she would go out of her way to be obliging.

I recently saw her having dinner with my wife after an operation, in my wife's bedroom. That kind of thing isn't done because of a lack of concern.

Everything interests her; peeves, among other things. And there's a lot of just chat which I sometimes simply come upon walking into a room and hearing conversations at my wife's end of the phone. So there's a lot of what I would call relaxed badinage.

*I'm not going to be like anybody else. I'm going to be Nancy Reagan.*

*The reason
she looks adoringly
at her husband
is because she adores him.*

She doesn't like anybody to criticize her husband. I think she feels that in the case of certain people, there's a sort of transcendent bond that allows certain liberties. George Will, for instance, was at the White House when we were watching *King Lear* with Laurence Olivier. That morning he'd written a very tough "anti-Reagan" piece. Still, the relationship was very civil. On the other hand, there's probably an interfaceable part of her memory that clocks these little things. I wouldn't be surprised, because she is the type. My wife is the same way.

Biologists tell you that every seven years we become completely renovated biological animals, and it is a continuing subject of scientific inquiry, the extent to which this biological change, the life and death of individual cells, affects your mind. I'm certain that if I were a clinical psychologist and I spent ten hours with her twenty years ago and ten hours with her tomorrow, I'd say there's been a change. But it's true of everyone. I don't see any change in her that reflects the fact she's the First Lady. The changes that I detect would be the changes that you would normally detect in a woman who was twenty years older than she was back then.

The reason she looks adoringly at her husband is because she adores him. The reason she is dressed chicly is because she dresses chicly. The reason for her rather delicate mannerisms is that that's the way she is. Whether she's at a ball or dressed in pajamas for breakfast in a beach house. That's just simply the ways she is.

*She doesn't like anybody to criticize her husband.*

Left: *Dinner for two in the family quarters, March 1984*

*She's a one-man woman. She lives, eats, and breathes for Ronald Reagan.*

## MICHAEL REAGAN

*I* think it's true that Nancy Reagan has grown in confidence and has come out more and become more assertive and happier, to an extent. I think the first term for everybody is rough. You're learning so much. Just learning to get around the White House in the first four years is tough enough. The only place she hasn't grown made my wife jealous. When she went into the White House, she was a size 6. She's now a size 4. And everybody wants her dresses.

I think it hurts Nancy to read negative things about herself or about anybody in the family, because sometimes they don't understand the whole story or the whole drift of what was going on, and so they're writing stories or saying things on television, not knowing all the facts.

I've talked to Dad about the same situation when I've picked up the paper and read something about myself. I'll just call Dad and say, "How can they say this?" Dad says, "Just don't worry about it. Let it roll off your back." She is thin-skinned, I think. She absorbs all that. Maybe it rolls off Dad's back; she's there and picks it up with a wheelbarrow.

She's a one-man woman. She lives, eats, and breathes for Ronald Reagan. And she is probably one of the most caring people in the world. She truly cares about family and home life. I think people misinterpret that sometimes as a coldness and it really isn't. She's just more caring than people realize. It's too bad some don't realize it as much as they should.

## BONITA GRANVILLE WRATHER

*I* think Nancy is a very special human being. And I think she was badly maligned in the early days in the White House by the press. They didn't know or didn't understand her. One thing that's always amazed me is that nobody has ever realized what a fantastic sense of humor she has. Her husband has one, too, of course, but people don't recognize that about Nancy.

I don't believe the media were willing to give her a chance in the beginning, though I think they are now. People realize that she is a very warm, sympathetic human being. I don't think people give her credit for how really intelligent she is, and always has been.

Nancy's anything but frivolous. She's very level-headed, she's very sincere, she's very down to earth, and why she seemed frivolous I don't know. Again, I'm going to blame it on the media. That very first year in the White House was a

pretty dreadful one. Not only the loss of her father, Loyal Davis, but that terrible attempted assassination. Her grief was private when her husband was hovering between life and death. Her grief was private when her father died. But once her husband recovered and they started going out, every time they stepped out of a car, every time they walked out of a door into the open, imagine the fear of being shot at. That would inhibit anyone. That first year was a very, very difficult one. It would have been for anyone.

I think everyone is hurt by criticism, especially if it's unfair. She's a very vulnerable lady and she's very sensitive. She responds to constructive criticism very well, but the unfair criticism hurt her terribly. I just hope now that she's toughened up enough to let unfair criticism roll off her back.

Left and below: *At the ranch.*

Right: *An early surprise Christmas present named Rex, 1985.*

## C.Z. WICK

*N*ancy Reagan has a terrific sense of humor, a terrific sense of style, is very giving, and is very tuned in to the world around her. She's willing to try new things, hear about new things. Above all, Nancy is interested in people, and fun to be with.

I think that the conservative characterizations of Nancy Reagan have missed the point of the person. She's a very curious person. She's a very open and interesting person, and not one to ignore the world around her. The single most fun thing that characterizes any gathering of our families, or just hanging out with her, is humor. She loves to laugh. She has a very quick sense of humor, and practical jokes and on-going family jokes are part of our relationship.

## RON REAGAN

*S*he's old-fashioned in some ways. She didn't grow up in the sixties or anything. She's from another era. She does think that it's better for my father to be out front alone. She's more comfortable that way. She's not as comfortable in the limelight as she is in the wings.

I guess she's a very sensitive person. She's a very private person and I think that's one reason why this has all been a little tough for her. She guards her privacy jealously, and doesn't like intrusions into that privacy. When they happen, her thin skin makes her react. It hurts her.

She can be a handful. I mean, she's not always the easiest person to get along with. I guess it's because of that sensitivity. She's a bit of a perfectionist. I don't think I'd want her to be my boss. I would guess she could be demanding as a boss because of that perfectionism.

She's an incredible phone person. She's always on the phone, ever since I was this big. We had to get more lines put in at home, to satisfy her.

Out at the ranch, Mom doesn't get up at daybreak and go bareback riding through the woods. She doesn't man the

*She's an incredible phone person. She's always on the phone, ever since I was this big. We had to get more lines put in at home to satisfy her.*

tractor or anything. She doesn't do the chainsaw, but she gets out there and neatens up the woods and stuff. I've seen her walk through woods and there'll be dead twigs hanging and she'll get up there and pull them off and kind of get the whole place so it's neat. She's not a big rider or a big outdoors person, not an athlete or anything like that, but she can't help but enjoy the ranch because my dad enjoys it so much and she derives a lot of pleasure from his enjoyment.

## MAUREEN REAGAN

She's exactly the same person she was the day she walked into the White House. We all grow, but inside ourselves. The things that we care about, our families and our friends and who we know and what we are, that doesn't change. I have been very upset at the idea that there is this new Nancy Reagan. It's not a new Nancy Reagan. A more confident Nancy Reagan. A more eloquent Nancy Reagan. But, gosh, I hope we're all more confident and more eloquent as years go by.

She's got this closet in the White House, and none of us are ever allowed to see it. She squirrels things away in this closet. Later, things come out of it. When my husband moved to Sacramento, she said, "Does he need a coffee maker?" I said, "Well, yeah, I think so." Rummage, rummage, rummage. We heard this sound, and all of a sudden, out comes a coffee maker.

Nancy Reagan was a career woman. She had a very good career in the motion-picture industry, and she got married. After she was married, she was offered one of the choice television roles of all time and turned it down, saying, "No, I want to raise a family, and I, personally, cannot do both. I know this about myself, and I don't want to take the chance of not being good at either by trying to do two things that I don't think I can put together." Her husband did not encourage her to leave her profession. It was her choice to make. In fact, he was really quite surprised.

## DOUG WICK

I've known Nancy Reagan since I was a kid. She's an old family friend. I went to grammar school with her kids. I think she's one of the great lunch dates in America. She's warm, smart, funny, a good friend. Needless to say, I like her.

Above: *Choosing a valentine at a Washington, D.C. card shop, 1986.*

*I don't think she's comfortable being the center of attention. She's someone who's more of a watcher, a person who's a little bit more comfortable on the sidelines, observing.*

She's an unusual combination of smarts—interesting, and a good listener. A lot of times people who have much to offer in one camp don't necessarily have a foot in the other, and she can do both. She's one of those rare people who, if you see her in a large group of people, when you speak to her, no matter where you are or who the group is, her eyes never leave your face. Her trick is that she also has that kind of antennae so she knows everything else that's going on in the room while she's talking to you; but she never does that kind of thing where you notice someone's eyes going over your shoulder to see who else is coming in.

I don't think she's comfortable being the center of attention. She's someone who's more of a watcher, a person who's a little bit more comfortable on the sidelines, observing. She seems to have very little interest about wanting to have everyone look at her.

The First Lady is an extremely complicated woman. When her husband first got into office, I don't think people really understood her. She's very shy, and that was misunderstood as maybe not caring or being aloof. As time has

gone on, people have gotten to know and understand her much better. In a funny way, because of the assassination attempt on her husband, they realized what a caring, deep, feeling person she is.

She's got unfailing instincts about people, and she's someone you can sit at a party with and she'll know everything that's going on in that room, including the kitchen. She can read someone from across the room. She knows who likes them, and who's trying to work some scam on one side or some scam on the other. In that way, I know the President trusts her judgment enormously.

I was working on the movie *Sophie's Choice,* and part of my job was to look for a Sophie—a blond Polish woman, a tragic figure. I thought Mrs. Reagan would be a good candidate, so I called her and asked her if she was interested, and she said it sounded like a pretty good job, but she had this whole other thing in Washington, and she'd have to see how she liked it. So, I bumped into her at the inauguration, and she came sweeping through with a giant entourage and I was in the crowd somewhere and she happened to catch my eye. She yelled across the room, "Keep Sophie on the back burner."

## NANCY REYNOLDS

*S*he was wounded by the early press criticism. It made her feel as if she was a sitting duck. Stories were filled with absolute lies in many cases, very prejudicial, skewed stories. I recall the reporters extremely well. I remember some of them, who today are famous authors

*She's got unfailing instincts about people, and she's someone you can sit at a party with and she'll know everything that's going on in that room, including the kitchen. She can read someone from across the room.*

*The First Lady's unexpected appearance at the Gridiron dinner of March 1982 marked a turnaround in her relations with the press.*

writing scathing accounts of their interviews of Nancy Reagan. She was totally bewildered, very deeply hurt. She herself feels that she was pleasant and being honest and had invited them into her home. Some would then come out with something that was just so totally off the wall. She was wary and it was not always easy to get her to do interviews. I think if you'd been slapped or stung a few times, you'd say, "Hey, I don't need this."

She's very funny. It's something that she shows privately to her friends and family. She's witty, very sensitive, very current on cultural things as well as on public affairs. She watches all the news broadcasts. She's well read. But she basically thinks of herself as a private person. Her loyalty is legendary. A few weeks after Ronald Reagan became governor, she was on an airplane going to Los Angeles, as she did every weekend, and she was sitting in the front seat and behind her were two men discussing Ronald Reagan's budget. They were criticizing the governor very loudly and you could see the steam beginning to build. Before you know it, she pushed her button and the seat slipped back and she turned around and said, "That's my husband you're talking about, and every bit of the information that you two are exchanging is wrong and incorrect. I would like the chance to correct you." Those two men were so stunned, they just sank about five inches in their seats. Their faces turned red and that was the last we heard from them.

If people ask her if she feels strongly about something, she certainly expresses herself. I've heard her many times disagree with the President and others. It's like everything else—you win some and you lose some. And she's done both.

It's true that sometimes, as a governor's wife, she would sit in the bathtub and rant and rave at people in private. Those of us who were on the staff could always tell when she'd had a bad day, because she would be in the bathtub having wonderful conversations, saying things to people whom she felt had been cool and unfair and really mean-spirited to her or to her husband or to her family. And it was one of the ways she blew off steam.

## SHEILA TATE

*S*he doesn't like surprises. No one would like to read in the paper that they felt this way or that way about something when they hadn't been consulted about how they really did feel.

She's a perfectionist. If you have failed to provide all the necessary information, then she's not going to feel secure about the event or the interview or whatever she's doing, so she will ask for more information.

I don't think it's a fair criticism that she demands when she should ask. I think that's from people who are unfamiliar with her way of doing things. Perhaps once they got a call and were so flustered that they stuttered and stammered.

Some say she gets along better with men than with women. She never ignored me. She certainly had close men friends, but I think she's interested in everybody.

## LYN NOFZIGER

*E*verybody wants to leave his or her own mark, but I believe she sees what she's doing really as a way of assisting the President, of building with him. We all have our own egos. But I don't think she's ever set out to have people compare her to him, or anything like that.

## MICHAEL DEAVER

*S*he's one of the most special people that I've ever known in the world. She's smart, she's strong, and very intense. She has a side to her that very few people know about. And that is this very strong personal loyalty to

*Ex-White House pet (and now ranch dog), "Lucky," gets a bath in the White House family quarters, April 1, 1985.*

*The First Lady models a "new hat" for the President, 1981.*

people who've been good to her, regardless of who they are.

I remember when my wife Carolyn's father died suddenly. We'd only been here three months. She called me on the phone and said, "Why don't you bring the kids up to Camp David for the weekend?" We got to Camp David, and she took those two kids of mine who had just lost their grandfather and made life wonderful for a weekend for them. She took them bowling, for hot dogs, bicycle riding, whatever they wanted to do. That's the side of Nancy Reagan nobody knows about. In California, during the Vietnam War, once a week, sometimes twice a week, without any press around, she'd quietly go to the Veterans' Hospital and sit there and hold a vet's hand, then go home and call their mothers and cry with them and go back the next week and do the same thing over again. She didn't do it because she was trying to change her public relations image. She was doing it because Nancy really cares about people.

## STUART SPENCER

*I don't think people realize that she is a vulnerable person.*

*I* don't think people realize that she is a vulnerable person. There was an article in the *Washington Star* during the 1980 campaign. It was a cheap shot. That woman was devastated for weeks. People talk about her being tough. They talk about her being involved in the process. Those things are all true, but she's also a vulnerable, sweet little person. A lot of her personal friends see that, but people in the political arena don't.

## DONNIE RADCLIFFE

*T*here is an element of the unapproachable about her. I would have hoped that after four years, with this particular press corps that follows her every move, there would be some feeling of rapport that has developed among us. I don't have that feeling. I believe we can have our differences and still have an understanding.

I mean, we might encounter her in a situation where she is walking toward members of the press she knows, and there is not a glimmer of recognition in her eyes. The President isn't that way. Sometimes he'll give you a little lift of the eyebrow, or a little wink. It doesn't mean that we've crossed each other's lines or we've succumbed to each other's charms, but it does mean that there is a human quality there that, with Mrs. Reagan, is missing.

I suppose she thinks she's been burned by the press and therefore she's wary. I don't know if she is really scared, and I do not necessarily suscribe to the view that she is timid and shy. I don't see Mrs. Reagan as that at all. I think she's more aloof and controlled about what the outer Nancy Reagan is.

I would like to like her. I really don't know whether I like her or not. I don't dislike her. I don't know that I would think of her as a close friend. I feel there's a certain detachment about her that makes it sort of difficult to feel a closeness to her. Now, she may be wonderful with her staff, but that's the sort of thing that doesn't get through to ordinary mortals. I still feel there's a curtain there.

I would like to feel that she is a warm, caring person, that I could go and talk about substantial things or concerns with her, but I don't know how that would ever be possible.

*...there's a certain detachment about her that makes it sort of difficult to feel a closeness to her.*

## JAMES ROSEBUSH

*Y*ou certainly don't have a person here who's changed herself to fit the occasion, but the experience of the past years has had an impact on her.

She was always willing to take risks—accept challenge—but now she does it with greater confidence. I think she takes all of the public acclaim now with a knock-on-wood attitude because she's not one to rest on those laurels. In the political world, they can evaporate. So I think she wants to work hard to keep the public confidence.

The First Lady is bright, she's hardworking, and she's good to work for in the sense that she knows what's going on.

She's very demanding of herself. You want to do your best for her. That's the way I respond to her. I want to do my best for her because she's demanding of herself and she expects good work out of people.

She likes to use the phone a lot more than I do. I've never been one to enjoy talking on the telephone, but that's her way of communicating with people. She's up there on the second floor of the White House, and you or I might get up and walk down to the office at the end of the hall to chew the fat with someone, but her way of communicating is on the telephone.

She has never once said to me, "Jim, you've overscheduled me. You've given me too much. You've made me climb too many flights of stairs." She's got boundless energy.

# DR. RICHARD DAVIS

*N*ancy came to Washington prepared—by parents, a good home, a fine education, and wonderful friends. Sometimes we forget that she was "First Lady of California" for eight years, so she did have experience when she arrived in Washington. I think the first two or three years in the White House caught her off stride. The first thing that threw her was some unfortunate press.

The second was the wounding of the President in March 1981. I remember that, of course, vividly. I had come down on several occasions, and three or four nights after his operation I visited the White House. Nancy had had a really dreadful day. Things were touch and go. We got back here and she seemed to shift gears. She actually took me on a little guided tour. We talked about different things, and finally the tour, so to speak, ended in a beautiful room on the third floor called the Solarium. It has a bay window and looks out over the Monument.

That night, though, it was under renovation and there weren't any lights in the room. It was early spring and the window boxes were filled with daffodils. Here we were standing in the darkness and there were these dancing yellow flowers, which represented to us, I guess, a hopeful future. We discussed a number of things. She expressed her gratitude about all the care the President had received from the doctors and nurses. And then she turned to me and said, "Now, Dick, my job this week is to really go over this room and renovate it so the President can recover here. It will make him feel like he's outside once again and, you know, we want to keep all that sunshine and happiness in his life."

And I thought that really was quite a remarkable thing. She showed no self-pity. She was thinking of a life probably more dear to her than her very own.

Left: *A surprise birthday cake at a news conference, 1984.*

*"Now, Dick, my job this week is to really go over this room and renovate it so the President can recover here. It will make him feel like he's outside once again and, you know, we want to keep all that sunshine and happiness in his life."*

# 3

# *Husband and Wife*

## NANCY REAGAN

*I* can't talk for anyone else. I can talk for me—what makes me happy, what makes my husband happy, what makes our marriage happy. For me, my husband and my family come first. And that makes me happy. I assume it makes them happy.

I think it's easier if you have a definite philosophy that you've held for a long time. I have a feeling that perhaps in the past, there've been some people who maybe haven't made up their minds clearly what their positions are, and that can age you pretty quickly. But if you have a pretty definite philosophy of what you want to do, then it makes things a lot easier.

Ron is that way, too. It's what he feels. He has his own instincts about what's right and what's wrong.

Do we ever fight? We disagree. We don't fight. Fight to me means throwing plates and all of that. There's nobody that you're going to agree with all the time, even your husband.

I'm often asked about thirty-three years of marriage, which today sounds like a long time. It doesn't seem like a long time, though. I got to thinking about it, and you're always reluctant to give anybody advice about marriage or how to have a long marriage or whatever, but I've really

*For me, my husband and family come first.*

been very lucky because most men or women, when they get married, like to feel that their husband or wife, if put to the test, if put under tremendous pressure, would act in a certain way, would act with great strength and make you very proud of them. You like to feel that. But very seldom does the average person have a chance to really see that husband or wife under those kinds of circumstances. I've been very lucky in that, because I've seen my husband under very pressured conditions. I know he's never failed. Never failed me. He's always stuck to principles. He's never done anything for purely political reasons. You go back to the assassination attempt. I don't know of many men who would have handled it that well.

## PRESIDENT REAGAN

How do you explain it? We're happy. I don't know how to answer it. From a man's standpoint, I could say what I think Clark Gable once said to someone, "There's nothing more important than approaching your own doorstep and knowing that someone on the other side of the door is listening for the sound of your footsteps."

I know that during the day, even before this job, whatever I was doing, something would happen in a day and the first thing that would go through my mind was picturing myself telling her about it when I got home.

We talk about everything. Sometimes, we disagree on someone or their particular qualifications or something, but never very seriously. It's good to talk about it and have other input. I feel better always knowing that we're in agreement.

*Right: Nancy and Ronald Reagan at the arrival ceremony for Premier Zhao of the People's Republic of China, January 1984.*

*From a man's standpoint, I could say what I think Clark Gable once said to someone, "There's nothing more important than approaching your own doorstep and knowing that someone on the other side of the door is listening for the sound of your footsteps."*

## MICHAEL REAGAN

don't think she advises him on decisions he makes as President. But it's important that Dad have her, because she is a sounding board for family feelings. She's an important part of his life. I've always said that, without her, Dad probably wouldn't be President of the United States. She gives him inner strength that he really needs, and that keeps him going every day, knowing that at the end of the day, he has her to go home to.

She sees the people around Dad and she wants them to be from the same mold they're from. I think that's what happens. She may voice an opinion on a person, whether they're doing the job and are looking the part they should play or not. She probably discusses that with Dad. But the ultimate decision on who he's going to have working with him is always up to Dad.

I think he values very much all the advice she gives him. Dad's just a stronger man because of Nancy Reagan, and she's been a very supportive force. Without her support, he would not have run for governor; he would not have run for President.

I think what pulled them through into the eighties was that Dad and the people around him wanted him to run. I

Right above: *The Republican National Convention, 1984.*

Right: *The First Lady interrupts preparations for the presidential debate at Camp David in October 1984.*

don't know if Nancy did. All of us were hurt after he lost to Ford at the end of '76. It was, What do you do, do you start this, do you do that? I think Dad's the one who pulled up his boots and said, No, we're going on. And then everybody supported him.

You make a negative remark about Ronald Reagan and Nancy's not going to be friendly to you. Her life really is centered around Ronald Reagan. She will do whatever is necessary to insulate him and keep him happy. She does her thing helping with the kids, with the grandparent program and the drug program, which are important to her, but, really, the most important thing to her is Ronald Reagan. So if you consider everything on that basis, then she isn't that complicated.

They do need each other. They both dance to the other one's tune. I mean, Dad is Nancy's strength in his way, and Nancy is his strength in the home life. I think they could live all by themselves and be perfectly happy. That's not to say that they don't want the kids or anything of that nature. But the fact is that now the kids are grown and gone, and their relationship hasn't changed in thirty years. They are the same people who met back in the fifties and got married in 1952. They haven't changed.

## WILLIAM F. BUCKLEY

*I* would say that, at one level, Nancy Reagan has total influence over her husband. That is to say I could not imagine his doing something which forfeited her loyalty or her devotion to him. But it would be very hard to imagine such a thing even in the abstract.

They are in every sense of the word companions. They share their thoughts, they share their peeves, they share their enthusiasms. And when something is brewing, it is coterminously communicated. It isn't something that he sort of announces. So there's never a situation in which all of a sudden he accosts her at noon and says, "Something's been cooking in my mind for three months. This is it." They just don't have that kind of relationship.

Suppose he asked Jimmy Carter to be special Mideast fixit man. Something like that he'd almost certainly discuss with her because of the bizarre character of it. But I can't believe he would discuss with her in any detail recommendations of who should be the new head of the Federal Reserve Board.

I think she has a very important role in the sense that he would never want to disappoint her, nor would he ever want

*They are in every sense of the word companions. They share their thoughts, they share their peeves, they share their enthusiasms.*

to surprise her. If, somewhere along the line, he decided to end the agriculture embargo, he'd know that doing so would at least annoy and, in some senses, outrage the hard anti-Communist part of his constituency. In a situation like that, it would be perfectly normal for him to discuss the consequences of an impending decision. It is very unlikely that she would weigh in during that discussion in such a way as to cause him to change his mind.

It's hard to say how good her instincts are because we don't often talk politics. We talk people. Take the whole matter of whether he would run in 1968. In that year there was an understanding, more or less, that if Nixon failed in the primaries in New Hampshire and Indiana, Reagan would come in rather than let Nelson Rockefeller have it. Of course, Nixon didn't fail in those primaries, but meanwhile a movement had developed. She was at once anxious for him to succeed in any enterprise and terribly afraid that he might be hurt. He didn't declare his candidacy until after he arrived in Miami, and at the time I was quite certain the reason he had finally entered the race wasn't because he thought there was any chance of winning it, but because he didn't want to let down people who had expended that much effort. She, in that situation, almost certainly urged him not to think so much about the people who had supported him as about himself.

They grew up in their early married life fighting Communists in Hollywood. It was a shared experience, one that

Right: *A visit at Bethesda after the President's cancer surgery, July 1985.*

Right above: *The first inauguration, January 20, 1981.*

*She believes he's absolutely unique. She probably thinks he belongs on Mount Rushmore. And any failure of the public to recognize this is a failure on its part to recognize that which is obvious to her.*

continues to be extremely strong in Reagan. And it helped form her opinions also.

There's a sense in which she's not that much of a hard-liner. He's very hard-line in his rhetoric, but less so in his actions. He's been softer on the Soviet Union in respect to Poland and Afghanistan than Carter was. I can't imagine a situation in which she would say to him, notwithstanding how he feels about the Soviet Union, "We have got to entertain Gorbachev when he comes over here." It's much more likely that he would accept the institutional requirements that he has as Chief of State and simply swing with it.

She believes he's absolutely unique. She probably thinks he belongs on Mount Rushmore. And any failure of the public to recognize this is a failure on its part to recognize that which is obvious to her. In that sense, she is more ambitious for him, but only because of her distinctive appreciation of him. Now is that the same kind of ambition that Lady Macbeth had, or is it something completely different? I think it's different. It's kind of a heliocentric relationship.

## BONITA GRANVILLE WRATHER

*N*ancy and Ronald Reagan are a team. They're devoted to one another, very much in love, and they work as a team and they always have. I understand it. Some people may not because they may not have husbands. My husband, until he passed away, was a partner of mine. We talked about everything. I can't say whether she gives him advice, but I think they talk about everything and they advise each other. When I hear people say, "Well, she's his adviser," that's not so. They just discuss things together.

I know that the President thinks his wife is a good judge of character, and that he values her opinion on everything, whether it's raising children or politics. It doesn't matter. He values her opinion. As, by the way, do all of her friends.

## C. Z. WICK

*W*hat I know well of their relationship is that she has excellent judgment, and, like any husband and wife, there's interest in what the other does. He knows he can rely on her very solid judgment, but I think that the character of that is his recognizing a smart person who is there for him and who's solid as a rock when he needs some good advice.

She has terrific instincts for people's motives and their personal agendas. She's micro and he's macro. He's the big

*Nancy and Ronald Reagan are a team. They're devoted to one another, very much in love, and they work as a team and they always have.*

Left: *Ten months into the first term, 1981.*

Below: *A toast at a Republican National Committee dinner, February 1984.*

Right: *Lighting the national Christmas tree, 1984.*

picture in terms of the whole country, while she's very good with the people who are close to him.

## RON REAGAN

She's got great instincts, not so much about what will play well to the country—that's where he comes in, that's where he's very good—but as to how he plays best, how he comes off best, under what circumstances, and in what surroundings.

I can't say whether he discusses things that are classified with her. I would guess he probably wouldn't want to. But they talk about everything else. They're very close. What don't you talk about with your wife?

## MAUREEN REAGAN

They have the ultimate relationship. They are each other's best friends. We all want to have that kind of relationship. They try things out on each other, using each other as sounding boards. There's a difference between

*They have the ultimate relationship.*

being an adviser and being somebody's best friend. He refines things that he's thinking about by saying them out loud and talking to her. She refines things she's thinking about in the same way, and they give each other advice in that way. They have always done that, and always will. They are absolutely a team. You do not get one without the other, ever.

There're always two parts to everything—the ideas, the ambition, the ability to do it. Then there's the rest of us behind the scenes who sort of make it all come together and make it all work. She has created an environment in their lives that allows him a lot of freedom to go out and explore things that he might not have under other circumstances. But I don't call that a driving force.

My initial reaction is that he would be President no matter what right now because I have a feeling of destiny about this particular enterprise. I think it all became possible because of the relationship they have, and because they both had a great deal of freedom, and because they have this incredible friendship that allows them to talk about things.

Left: *A walk during a quiet moment of the Geneva Summit, November 1985.*

## NANCY REYNOLDS

*N*ancy Reagan's only interest is what's good for the President. She has no hidden agenda, no other worries or concerns. She feels that if there are people who have other agendas—and in politics there are always such people—they are definitely working at some sort of disadvantage to the President and she's going to speak up.

They certainly fulfill each other's needs, and perhaps that's the basis for a really successful marriage. They communicate with one another extremely well. And they have such mutual admiration and respect for one another. Based on those two things, they agree on most issues. They share so many things in common, but mostly they fulfill each other's needs, most of the personal needs we all have. He loves and respects her very much, and vice versa. Like most marriages, no one is ever giving fifty-fifty. At one time or another someone has done the eighty-twenty bit or ninety-ten. They've each had an opportunity to be in that position, as partners in all good relationships do. And I think they have the bond, a personal bond, of all the things they've gone through together. It has only strengthened over the years.

## SHEILA TATE

*F*irst of all, if you know Nancy and Ronald Reagan, you know that he's not going to ever consider her a liability. She's his biggest asset, emotionally, and we knew we could get that story out [to the press].

To some degree, I think she was a convenient lightning rod, and when you have a popular President, it's hard to attack him. His wife is vulnerable. People took shots at her.

They're inextricably bound together, but she's certainly carved out an independent niche for herself that she can be proud of in her own right. I think she's probably teased the President about the fact that her rating is sometimes a little higher than his.

Do I feel she's a little competitive with the President? Only on the friendliest basis. We'd say, "We were the lead story on the network news," and she'd say, "I can't wait to tell Ronnie."

She was probably the best person to address the issue of the President's age. She'd been through it before. She's the closest person there is to the President and she knew that it was not an issue. We were out campaigning and she took that issue head on. She would walk over the rope lines when we'd get to an airport and invite reporters' questions, and she

would welcome that particular one. She had a very good sense that she could address that question in a way probably no one else could.

## LYN NOFZIGER

*N*ancy's a perfectly normal human being. When things go wrong with her husband, and she thinks somebody's at fault, she gets upset. Then she gets over it. She's protective of him, and that's a good thing. I'm sure all she's concerned about is that the people who work for him serve him well. That's what she's concerned about.

She's more interested in public relations and the President's popularity than she is, let's say, in his sticking to conservative doctrine. Apparently people want it both ways. Nancy goes with what is best for Ronald Reagan, and certainly part of that is, Does he adhere to his principles? We all of us look at the public relations side of it. That's part of politics. But I don't think that she does that to the exclusion of principle.

She is a very important woman. I don't think she's uncomfortable. She feels very strongly that her husband is the President and that he's the man who ought to be taking the credit, the person who ought to be out in front. To that degree, she has put herself somewhat in the background, but that's not an unusual thing for a woman to do.

## ED ROLLINS

*I*think she is a constant adviser. She is without question his closest friend. She certainly doesn't try to get involved in the day-to-day policy decisions, but I think there's no question that when he wants someone whose advice he trusts, he goes to her.

He certainly likes it when she reinforces him. When she disagrees with him, he probably really ponders whether he's going in the right direction or not. So I would certainly say he heeds her advice.

She has as much clout as she wants. If she wants to weigh in on something, it certainly becomes the focus of his agenda, and can certainly become the focus of a lot of other attention around the White House.

Ronald Reagan is to a certain extent a very solitary man. He's unique. He has no ego. He has no need for friends or advisers or what have you. He's just very comfortable with himself. And there's one person in that inner circle, day

*I think she is a constant adviser. She is without question his closest friend.*

Below: *Air Force One, February 22, 1981.*

Right: *The Reagans celebrate their thirty-third wedding anniversary, March 1985.*

in and day out, one person who's a constant, whose judgment he values above all. I think that makes her an extremely important part of the team.

I think the President's toughness is totally underestimated. He has a real inner toughness—when it comes down to things that are really crucial and important, he's there on the line. It's easier for her to make judgments because she's not dealing face-to-face with people the way he is. When a staff person is not serving the President well, the President may still like that person. She's in a little more of an abstract situation. She can make judgments based on performance, where sometimes other factors enter into the President's judgment.

She can be very tough, no question about it.

I don't think he can rely on her any more than he does. He relies on her so much already. The President has had a career—not just his political career but his movie career—in which there have been a lot of people in and out. Making movies, he's had different directors, different co-stars. But for over thirty years, the one constant in his life has been her. Ronald Reagan would be very happy on his mountain top, all alone, with one exception—he'd like to have her with him.

*For over thirty years, the one constant in his life has been her. Ronald Reagan would be very happy on his mountaintop, all alone, with one exception— he'd like to have her with him.*

## RICHARD ALLEN

The President is the kind of man who, from my observation, in dealing with this able and strong-willed wife, recognizes that she's on his side all the time. He's able to listen carefully and maybe it influences his point of view and maybe it doesn't. He doesn't always give expression to whether he approves of what you're doing, saying, or how you're behaving. It's a very interesting feature of the man.

To see Ronald and Nancy Reagan in circumstances of difficulty, as I have seen them in the pre-campaign days and campaign days when things looked pretty dark at one point, and to watch them operate at the White House, one sees a reflection of a relationship that is clearly, in the first instance, grounded in love and caring about each other. The fact of the matter is that the President misses her if she's away twenty-four or forty-eight hours. It's almost an unbreakable team effort.

There are lots of things that a husband will not want to do in which a wife can help out without her work carrying the connotation of dirty work. I think that's very helpful. I'm pushed frequently by my wife and I think he is pushed frequently by his wife to do things or not to do things.

She steps into a role that he probably at least subconsciously invites her to fill. I think that's very interesting. Every couple that is married knows about those limits on either side. Most husbands invite their wives in. Others do not and live to regret the day. I think President Reagan has invited Nancy Reagan into that realm. She knows what the margin is, the boundary, so to speak, and she operates freely up to that boundary.

## MICHAEL DEAVER

Nancy will fight to her dying day to protect Ronald Reagan, whether he's actor, governor, private citizen, or President. She wants to know, Is he getting out on the patio for lunch to get some of that sunshine? What's he having for lunch today? Don't you give him some time in the morning? Give him some time in the afternoon so that he can sit at his desk and think a little bit himself. She is not the kind of person who would call up and say, "You know, I think the SALT talks ought to begin February second." Her primary concern would be his personal needs.

I'm married. Sometimes I win, sometimes Carolyn wins. The same is true of the Reagan household, as it is in most

*She wants to know, Is he getting out on the patio for lunch to get some of that sunshine? What's he having for lunch today? Don't you give him some time in the morning? Give him some time in the afternoon so that he can sit at his desk and think a little bit by himself.*

households. Sometimes they argue and she'll prevail, and sometimes he'll prevail, but it's the most incredible love relationship I've ever seen in my life between a couple.

I suppose anybody who's here wants to leave something of themselves as far as their own mark and I'm sure that's probably true of Nancy. I've said this before. If Ronald Reagan had owned a shoe store, she'd be out there pushing shoes.

## DR. BARBARA KELLERMAN

Nancy Reagan's greatest strengths and greatest weaknesses have the considerable charm of being one and the same. Her greatest strength is that she is so tied to her husband she provides him with the kind of emotional support all of us wish we had. Her greatest weakness is that she is so tied to her husband and she provides him with so much emotional support that I think she is relatively ill-equipped to stand back and say, "You're doing this wrong. You might want to take another look at this."

Don't look to Nancy Reagan to provide Ronald Reagan with a critical perspective. On the other hand, do look to Nancy Reagan for this enduring emotional support.

If we had access to the living quarters, even if we were a fly on the wall of the Reagan apartment in the White House, I think it would be very hard for us to understand fully what goes on. I think in a relationship between two people, one doesn't see orders being given. It's a dynamic, the way all relationships are dynamic. I don't for a moment believe Nancy Reagan orders her husband to do this or do that. She makes her opinions felt in certain ways, the way all women and men do in the context of long marriages and long relationships. Those opinions, in a good marriage, in a good relationship, will be taken very seriously by the other person. It's that kind of power: power that's private; power that's abstract, if you will; power that's articulated much more through interpersonal influence than it is through the usual kinds of authority relationships we associate with the word "power."

*If Ronald Reagan had owned a shoe store, she'd be out there pushing shoes.*

# 4

# First Lady

## NANCY REAGAN

*I* hope people like me. I think it's been a process of getting to know me, and that took a long time. Probably some of it was my fault, some theirs. It was so new to me. I didn't know quite what to do, and there's no training for this job. When something is new to me, and I'm a little shy about doing something, then I tend to hold back.

The first year was a bad year for lots of reasons. I had all these personal problems that were on my mind and I was holding back.

There wasn't a deliberate sitting down and saying, "Now I've got to turn this around." It wasn't that. I'm no different than I ever was. But as time went on, I became more used to the job, and more used to being here. I got past the first year.

I always knew I wanted to be involved in the drug problem, and then I had more time. I was more ready for it, and it just evolved.

There isn't any clearly defined role for the First Lady. You make of it what you want. I see my role as doing what I'm doing. I didn't realize that you had such a tremendous platform, that if you were interested in one particular thing, you could try to advance it and inform people and get your

*It was so new to me. I didn't know quite what to do, and there's no training for this job.*

feelings across. I've chosen that way. But then, everybody has their own way.

The term "the right image" seems to me such a phony kind of staged thing—I'm going to carve out this image and that's what I'll be. Now, whatever kind of image that conjures up in people's minds, I don't know. But all I can do is be myself. I'm not going to be like anybody else. I'm going to be Nancy Reagan. So I'll push the things that I'm interested in. That's the way it's been all through history. Every First Lady has her own particular style or her own particular individuality and gets her own particular criticism.

Is it true I can be "relentless"? I think I know what I want. But, actually, I would think that if I were working for somebody, I would rather work for a person who knew what she wanted. The other would be very confusing to me. I wouldn't know if this is what she wanted or if that's what she wanted.

We have a lot of laughs, though if I'm upset about something that somebody's done, I tend to just pull back. A curtain comes down. Now I don't know whether that's good or bad, but that's always been so. I don't yell and shout and throw things, I just pull back.

*All I can do is be myself. I'm not going to be like anybody else. I'm going to be Nancy Reagan.*

*Everybody who's been here knows the job's tough.*

Everybody who's been here knows the job's tough. I would never criticize another First Lady. I never knew that Mary Lincoln was criticized so terribly. Well, she was. Across the hall, there's a painting of Mrs. Coolidge. It's a beautiful painting, her standing with their dog. She was criticized because supposedly there were people who said that her dress was really shorter than it was—it was really kind of a flapper style—and that she had had it painted on and added to and it was not the dress at the Smithsonian. There was a whole big flap about this. Mrs. Lincoln was criticized for spending $2,000 on her inaugural gown. Criticism comes with the job.

I don't think I'm getting all that bad a press now. I think as things have settled down and people have gotten to know me more, they know that a lot of things were not true.

I hear a lot of times, "Well, Nancy Reagan wants this, or Nancy Reagan wants that," when I've never said anything about it and I don't know what they're talking about.

Does the President sometimes say no to me? Sure. Does his no always end it? Not always. I'll wait a little while; then I'll come back at him again.

Above: *Answering some mail about the anti-drug campaign.*

Right: *At a state dinner held in his honor, Ecuadoran president León Febres-Cordero speaks to Nancy and Secretary of State George Schultz (center), January 1986.*

It really reaches a point where something's gone much too far, in my opinion. So it seems to me, sometimes, that if you can catch it before it reaches that point where a lot of people are maybe hurt, then it's easier to stop it right in the beginning, rather than let it build up a head of steam.

I don't have as much "clout" as they say I do. I don't get involved in how to balance the budget or how to reduce the deficit or foreign affairs or whatever, but I do get involved in people issues. I think I'm aware of people who are trying to take advantage of my husband, who are trying to end-run him.

Sometimes he'll want to talk about problems and sometimes he won't. Sometimes his mind is so busy and so occupied, he just wants to go right to those papers as soon as he gets his dinner. And then, there's not much conversation about it. Other times, he does want to talk about it.

I didn't think it was fair when I'd pick up the paper and I'd read that he was a warmonger, that he was ready to go to war and so on. I know that that's simply untrue. He's trying to do everything he can to avert war and bring about peace. That concerns me too. I was in favor of a meeting with Gromyko. I thought that was a good idea, and I'm glad he came.

He and my husband were over at the Oval Office alone and, having dismissed everybody else, I was asked to come down to the Red Room and be there to greet them when they got back. They came in, and we said hello, and they came

*I don't have as much "clout" as they say I do... but I do get involved in people issues. I think I'm aware of people who are trying to take advantage of my husband, who are trying to end-run him.*

around with the trays. He took some tomato juice or something, I took a Perrier, and he toasted me and I toasted him and then it was just sort of small talk. I think we were talking about the metric system. He turned and looked at me and said, "Is your husband in favor of peace or war?" And I said, "Peace." And he said, "Are you sure?" And I said, "I'm sure." And he said, "Well, then, you whisper 'Peace' in his ear every night." And I said, "I will. I'll also whisper it into your ear."

I haven't much time to be lonely. We plunged into so many things right away, there isn't time. When we went to church one Sunday, my husband said, "Look at this schedule. It used to be so simple just to go to church. All we're doing is going to church, and look at all these people who are involved." Or, if we go to Camp David, he'll say, "What are all those helicopters doing out there?" You know, he still can't get over it that everything takes so many people around you.

I think he's happy. He enjoys being in the position of being able to try to do the things he feels very strongly about and has for a long time. Yes, I think he's happy.

Sometimes, it's very hard. At this particular time, with what's happening worldwide and certainly in this country, with the deficit and so on. Tremendous.

Being governor of California was very good training for this job, particularly because, as he said often during the campaign, he came in as governor when the state was in almost the same position as the country. It was broke financially and so on. You just multiply that by I don't know how many times. Of course, California didn't have a foreign policy.

It's more work than I thought it would be, for me. I can't speak for him. He brings back stacks of papers that he reads every night, in his study or the living room, whatever, until he falls asleep at eleven-thirty or midnight. And he gets frustrated by the entrenched bureaucracy—because it's an entrenched bureaucracy.

I have moments of accepting that my husband is President, and then moments of thinking I'm not really here. I was interested when Prime Minister Thatcher was here. She said somewhat the same thing to my husband. She said, "Do you ever have times when you think of other heads of state and you think, oh, they must be so brilliant, so marvelous, and so extra special? And then you realize that you're a head of state, and you think, I'm just an ordinary person."

There was a tremendous emotional upheaval that I didn't count on—at leaving our home and our children. I'm sure you saw the picture of Pattie and some others at the house crying. And my crying. There was all this extra in it

*Right below: Interview with Liz Owen of* Life *magazine, November 1982.*

*Above right: With President and Mrs. Campins of Venezuela, 1981.*

that I really hadn't counted on. All of it together did get me down for a while.

But I'm enjoying it. Yes, I am enjoying it.

## LETITIA BALDRIDGE

he First Lady belongs to the people. She has thousands of letters addressed to her every month, asking for advice, consolation, help. What she does is reflected throughout the entire United States. If she has good posture, mothers say to their daughters, "Stand up straight. Don't you see Mrs. Reagan has good posture?" If she has a good figure, everyone wants to look like her. If she has a beautiful home and has good taste, everyone wants to have the same apricot-color living room that she has, and banana yellow on the walls. Everyone wants to copy the First Lady.

Therefore, if she is intelligent and if she has style and grace, it's pretty nice to copy someone like that. She also is a wonderful helpmate to her husband, a true partner. And although she doesn't make policy decisions, the mere fact that she is the ultimate sympathetic ear at night when the President of the United States returns to his private quarters is very important.

It's impossible to please all the public. But things straighten out through the years. Various First Ladies have

*The First Lady belongs to the people. She has thousands of letters addressed to her every month asking for advice, consolation, help.*

*I doubt there's a man alive who
is in love with his wife and doesn't
trust her intuition. She sees a
lot on her own, I'm sure, that the
President doesn't.*

been criticized for being overly involved in White House affairs. People forget that and remember them for their intelligence. I think Mrs. Reagan is establishing a very classic, wonderful path, lending a supportive ear to her husband but not even pretending to interfere in public policy.

I doubt there's a man alive who is in love with his wife and doesn't trust her intuition. She sees a lot on her own, I'm sure, that the President doesn't. I think it's good to have that kind of advice.

I think she will go down in history as one of the very finest First Ladies because she has gone through bad publicity and surmounted it so beautifully. She has done such wonderful things with her drug program, her foster child program, and so forth. She's been involved in a lot of things. She is working hard on the drug program at a time when drug and alcohol abuse is really a very serious problem in this country. She's right on target. And what she does is very effective. She has influence. She works hard at it. I think she also derives great satisfaction from seeing the good that she does.

There's a growth process in every First Lady. I've seen it in every single one of them. Mrs. Ford went through great personal problems and rose to surmount them. Rosalynn Carter and Lady Bird Johnson, wow, I mean Lady Bird does things to this day. She has power and influence in the whole field of world wildlife and preservation that she never would have had if she hadn't been First Lady and if she hadn't evolved during her years as First Lady.

Mrs. Reagan has evolved, too. If they are smart, intelligent women, if they have their eyes and ears open, and they don't succumb to prejudices, all First Ladies evolve and become greater people. If nothing else, they don't get any money out of it, and though they get a lot of grief out of it, they also develop inwardly and store up a tremendous amount of knowledge. It must affect their whole lives for ever and ever. Once you're out of the White House, a First Lady has to be very changed and has to be very involved in what's going on around her. Just think of all the newspapers they suddenly start to read.

When you're that busy, you don't have time to give in to grief. You just keep plowing ahead. That's one of the perks of the job. You've so many things you have to do. There's this enormous schedule laid out for you. You don't have time to dwell on grief or sadness or fear. You just push ahead and do your job. And I think that's what she's done. First Ladies have to realize that when they come into the job—Claire Luce had a marvelous expression—"no good deed goes unpunished." They keep doing good deeds for the White House, for their country, and they're constantly criticized

Left: *The state visit of Egyptian president Anwar Sadat and Mrs. Sadat in August 1981.*

*Claire Luce had a marvelous expression—"no good deed goes unpunished."*

for it. But you have to go ahead and keep on anyway.

Both Mrs. Reagan and Mrs. Kennedy are remarkably good-looking, remarkably kind and motherly in many ways. The two of them can be compared a great deal. What makes Mrs. Reagan so unique is the wonderful love affair that she has with her husband. They're like young lovers. It's wonderful to see them walk down the hall hand in hand. I keep reminding my husband that we never hold hands. The Reagans hold hands all the time. And I think America loves that. It's a great, great symbol of marriage.

It's very hard when you're working your utmost to do the right thing in your job, and you're giving it your all, to see it put in the headlines as something negative. It's very frustrating. Of course she was hurt and frustrated in the beginning and, intelligent woman that she is, she learned to accept it, to expect it, and not to be bothered by it. You have a choice in the White House: you either have a complete nervous breakdown or you learn to forget it. And that's what she has done.

Mrs. Johnson came along in history at just the right moment, because the youth started to revolt and the women's movement began. And women started leaving the home in

*At Senator Edward Kennedy's home in McLean, Virginia, for a fundraising effort for the John F. Kennedy Memorial Library.*

droves to go to work. She was such an executive, the women related to her and were inspired and encouraged by her. When Mrs. Reagan came into the White House, there was a tremendous need for the whole subject of husband and wife to be seen in a new light. People were putting each other down and the new young woman executive was perhaps too aggressive. All of a sudden, here was an old-fashioned family coming back into the White House. It was a great moment for that to happen because not only was she a fantastic wife but she also developed these programs of her own.

The whole idea of husband and wife plus the woman who does not work but involves herself in the non-profit sector in a very meaningful way, it all came along at the right time in history. The First Lady is always a role model for women, whether she likes it or not, and whether they like it or not, they look up to her. And what she does is very important to all the young women who are getting their MBAs and to women who are trying to save their marriages and all of this. It's of tremendous sociological importance.

I think there were more women who applauded her, coming back with some of the old-fashioned, more conservative values at a time when we needed them. America's feminist movement has taken such great strides and has gone forward so fast that the whole subject of having children and being married needed paying attention to. And she's done it.

## NANCY REYNOLDS

Nothing prepares you for being First Lady, nothing. Basically, Washington is not a city that wishes you well. So I think you come in here really unprepared for the onslaught of personal and press criticism. Mother Theresa could be in the White House and within six months there would be some sort of exposé story about something she had done.

In Nancy Reagan's case, she is a woman who always takes things a day at a time. She concentrates entirely on one project, and her own personal concerns about the President's welfare come at the top of the list. Getting settled in the White House, making it a home, not just a public house, was a very important thing for her. So she concentrated on getting the house the way she wanted it and making it a comfortable, warm, and welcoming place for the President at the end of the day.

She's always been like that. I think she was just totally unprepared for the fact that people expected, as they often do unrealistically, a kind of First Lady who was going to leap into a project immediately and become something they

*Nothing prepares you for being First Lady, nothing. Mother Teresa could be in the White House and within six months there would be some sort of exposé story about something she had done.*

*What happens in Washington is that people try to push projects on you. Nancy Reagan has her own best instincts about what she wants to do, how it's going to work for her, and the kind of time she's going to give it.*

felt she should be. Now Nancy Reagan has always had a couple of projects in the years I've known her. The Foster Grandparent program and preventing drug abuse have been the two things that she's always been interested in, always put time in on. When she got to Washington, she wanted to continue with the Foster Grandparent program because she knew it, she felt comfortable in it, she had really put her mark on it all those years, and had done extraordinary things for the program.

What happens in Washington is that people try to push projects on you. Nancy Reagan has her own best instincts about what she wants to do, how it's going to work for her, and the kind of time she's going to give it. She felt that, except for the Foster Grandparent program and her interest in the drug program, she wanted to take a little time and see what was ahead. I think she became buried in the details and interests of what to do in the White House, managing a large staff. She had never been a manager before. All of her staff were new people—from her press secretary to her social secretary—people she had just met. I think it was kind of overwhelming at first. So she was unprepared for good old Washington and the immediate criticism that comes your way if you're not conforming to Washington's rules of how they think the First Lady should behave.

Her performance at that Gridiron dinner changed her image; most certainly the President's near death did. The assassination attempt had a tremendous effect on her, as had her own father's death. All of these things coming in the first year. All of them were traumatic, although the Gridiron was fun.

People always ask, "Has Nancy Reagan changed?" She really has not. What has changed is the perception of her. For years and years and years, we had all been saying, here's this wonderful, witty, funny, caring, loyal, intensely dedicated woman, but no one ever wanted to hear it. I attended thousands of press briefings and listened to hundreds of press women interviewing her over the years. In the sixties, in Sacramento, you were dealing with young, sixties reporters, most of them ardent feminists who came in with a chip on their shoulder, already making up their minds, and with a very cynical view of a First Lady who cared about her family first and foremost.

She is not someone who likes to make speeches or public appearances unless it's on behalf of her particular interests. I think she was a nervous wreck, appearing before the Gridiron. You never know how it's going to come off. But it showed the side of her that we've all known for years. You could feel the difference in the audience. You could feel people judging her very differently from this woman they had

*State visit of King
Fahd of Saudi Arabia
in February 1985.*

made casual assumptions about. She turned out to be something quite different.

She's a very complex person sometimes. She has many sides to her, and this was a side no one had ever seen. And when she did the encore, you knew she was having fun. You can sense when people approve of what you're doing. The applause was tremendous. That one incident showed that she basically has excellent instincts about herself and what she feels will be good and what will be natural for her. She never extends those boundaries by trying to do something that isn't natural, that isn't something she would do in ordinary life. Poking fun at herself at the Gridiron dinner was her way of perhaps saying, Well, if I got off to a rocky start, let's have a few laughs about it because I'm going to be around for a while. I think that was the turning point. There's no question about it.

*I don't think on substance that you can say Nancy Reagan has influenced policy. She expresses herself as we all do to the President when we have the opportunity. He always listens very intently. Of course, he adores Nancy.*

I don't think on substance that you can say Nancy Reagan has influenced policy. She expresses herself as we all do to the President when we have the opportunity. He always listens very intently. Of course, he adores Nancy. Many times she's right and he's not right. At least we feel that way. But sometimes he will accede if he feels that it's something he hasn't thought about. It's more style than substance. She never claims to be an expert. She certainly is knowledgeable and understanding about a lot of things, but Nancy Reagan is a back-to-basics person.

I think she sees her husband as a man of peace. He *is* a man of peace. To that end, I think she will always offer up solutions and ideas and comments, as we all do any time we're asked, and even sometimes when we're not.

But Ronald Reagan is his own man. I think she has influence in the general sense, but any wife of all those years is going to have an opinion. And his daughter Maureen, who spends a great deal of time at the White House, most certainly has a lot of influence. He doesn't always agree with her, either. That's what makes it such an interesting family.

When I first met Nancy Reagan, she was a housewife in her forties who had never been on the campaign trail before. Ronald Reagan had done a lot of campaigning for Senator Goldwater, and she had stayed home as most wives do and loved being in that rather protected environment. To be thrust all of a sudden into Sacramento and asked to live in an old mansion that was a firetrap and not near any schools—that was a big story in those days, that Nancy

*A toast from Chinese Premier Zhao, January 1984.*

*Barbara Bush and the new First Lady applaud President Reagan's inaugural address while the former administration looks on.*

Reagan said the governor's mansion wasn't good enough for her. In fact, it wasn't safe enough. The fire department said there was no way they'd ever get off that second floor if a fire came along. The wood was rotting. It was in an awful neighborhood. Now it's a museum.

So she insisted on moving to a suburb. That sounds a little silly now, but in those days, it was pretty courageous. She took a lot of flak from the press on that. She wanted a normal life for her children, especially for her young son, and in a neighborhood, in a house, that looked just like all the other houses. That was what she wanted. Ultimately, it was the best thing. But you're damned if you do and damned if you don't. I think she found out the hard way. These things all made sense to her. She really couldn't understand that anybody wouldn't agree that it was a sensible thing to do.

Nancy Reagan never held a press conference the whole time she was in Sacramento. She felt it was presumptuous. There were a few incidents where she had press in or something, but she never really called a press conference, except for one time. That was when a man who was a leader of the opposition in California publicly criticized her for trying to solicit furniture for a governor's mansion that wasn't even built. She was trying to get people to donate antiques or old California pieces, and there was a big, critical piece in the paper. She called a press conference the next day and just absolutely let him have it. It was the only time I ever saw her do that. She had her dander up and she felt that they had gone far enough. That was the end of the criticism. There was never another article, and she got tremendous donations of furniture and antiques from people who wanted to give them to the state to be used in a governor's mansion in the right way.

## DR. BARBARA KELLERMAN

*T*here's no set definition for the role of First Lady. The role as realized at any given moment in time really depends largely on three separate factors. One is the woman who's filling it. Two is the man she's married to. And three, by no means the least important, is the temper of the times. One can predict that a First Lady in the nineteen-eighties will be different from a First Lady in the fifties.

There are lots of common denominators among First Ladies, and in powerful ways the role has stayed remarkably the same as it was twenty and thirty years ago.

There was one First Lady who deviated somewhat from the norm in our recent history and that was Rosalynn

*There's no set definition for the role of First Lady.*

Carter. Jimmy and Rosalynn Carter were very close before they entered the White House. They were certainly well matched and partners, in effect, during the four years that they were in the White House. But Rosalynn Carter always took a very strong interest in the substance of her husband's political life. If that's your interest as First Lady, then the nature of the relationship and the nature of what you talk about and how you decide to spend your time—literally, how your days are spent—will differ enormously than if you are more like Nancy Reagan, which is to say, less interested in substance and more interested in being protective of her husband, as we know her to be.

Rosalynn Carter was interviewed in the White House by Barbara Walters. She was asked questions on policy matters. She was asked about energy, about health, about the political situation. You will notice that when Nancy Reagan is interviewed, there's rarely a question directed at her about any substantive policy issues.

This is not to say that, in the privacy of their own quarters, they don't discuss these issues. But I think it's safe to guess, from the evidence that we have, that she's not as interested in these matters as her predecessor was. Rather, she sees it all through a political lens of sorts, that is, how it will politically affect the well-being of her husband. That should not be lightly dismissed, because White House life is political life.

I think Nancy plays a large role with regard to personnel matters, though I don't believe she plays a larger role than other First Ladies have—compared, let's say, to Rosalynn Carter, which is the most obvious comparison because they've been the most powerful First Ladies of recent times. Anyone who reads the newspapers knows that Nancy Reagan helps her husband make decisions with regard to who should be around him, and when somebody lets her husband down and gets him into trouble—we have some recent evidence of so-called sloppy staff work—there are immediately reports that Nancy Reagan is furious at this and is doing everything she possibly can to make sure it doesn't happen again.

If you're going to look at the recent First Ladies, they really need to be viewed in their own separate categories. In different ways, they all exerted power.

Jacqueline Kennedy certainly was divorced from the political life of her husband. On the other hand, she was so attractive a figure, such a star in the White House, that her aura, by osmosis, almost lent him an aura of sorts. To be a media celebrity is to exert a kind of political clout, even if that clout is only in terms of public relations.

Lady Bird Johnson was for many years—in fact, during the entire Johnson marriage—what I call his trusted and in-

*If you're going to look at the recent First Ladies, they really need to be viewed in their own separate categories. In different ways, they all exerted power.*

dispensable junior business partner. She was junior because she knew or felt herself to be junior and never claimed to be his equal the way Rosalynn and Jimmy would say, "We're partners."

At the same time, she was always engaged in his political life, indispensable to his political life, and remained so in the White House. So her clout during her husband's White House tenure derived from various political activities she undertook on her own. For example, during the 1964 campaign, there was the "Lady Bird Special," which was one of the first efforts by a First Lady to step out on her own, to campaign alone, and to really become a political figure in her own right.

She also had her own projects. She had highway beautification and conservation and so forth and so on. Through Lyndon Johnson's dependence on her, through her long historical ties to his political career, and through her own projects—in at least three ways—she played a political role.

Pat Nixon's political clout was perhaps less than that of any of the other recent First Ladies. Basically, there are two ways to be politically powerful in the White House or to have some political impact there. One is through your tie to your husband, like Nancy Reagan's; and the other is to be such an attractive, imposing, or impressive figure in your own right that you get media attention and political attention the way Jacqueline Kennedy did. Pat Nixon, although she was attentive politically, and played her role capably and well, simply didn't have that strong a relationship with her husband. Nor was she so attractive, to those interested in political life and political culture, that she derived any clout from that. So she had less of an impact than other First Ladies.

Betty Ford is a separate story. The Fords entered the White House in a very unusual way. There was no campaign. Virtually overnight, they were catapulted from relative obscurity into the White House. She played a very important role in those early months, making him better known, attracting attention in her own right. Shortly after they entered the White House, she developed breast cancer. She was very open about her breast cancer, which other women in public life had not been up to that moment. From that point on, she became rather a loved figure. When he ran for President, for what really amounted to the first time, in 1976, buttons began appearing: "Betty's Husband in the White House" or "Betty for President." She really became a very popular First Lady, and in many ways deservedly so.

What the public expects from a First Lady depends on the temper of the times. It's a difficult balancing act nowadays because we all live in a very different time with

*What the public expects from a First Lady depends on the temper of the times. It's a difficult balancing act nowadays because we all live in a very different time with regard to women and what women are supposed to do and what we expect.*

Above: *The First Lady's trip to China resulted in a campaign to raise funds to save the endangered panda population in the People's Republic.*

regard to women and what women are supposed to do and what we expect.

Nancy Reagan's experience as First Lady is somewhat atypical. The more conventional pattern for First Ladies, and indeed for presidential families and presidents, is for everyone associated with a new administration to have something of a honeymoon, and this extends to the President's wife. People are usually withholding judgment. For whatever reason, Nancy Reagan's career as a First Lady has been reversed. She was under attack much more during the first year than she has been since, and appears to be in much better shape now with regard to her public appearances and her appreciation by the public than she was in the beginning.

The interesting question to ask about Nancy Reagan is exactly how she reversed the trend. I think you have to look at the three critical factors, the three pieces of the "First

Lady Puzzle." One is Nancy herself. She is much more comfortable now as First Lady than she was in the beginning. She's more relaxed. She's less defensive, less self-protective, and has simply gotten accustomed to the role in a way she was not at the very beginning. Second, there's the trajectory of her husband's career. In the very beginning, the Reagans were an unknown quantity—Washington outsiders. No one knew how this so-called B movie actor from Hollywood would fare in the White House. I think the evidence has been that he has had in many ways a remarkably successful presidency. And his 1984 electoral victory is evidence of the fact that he is widely admired, liked, respected. People enjoy having him in the White House. If you enjoy having a particular President in the White House, you are also enjoying having the First Lady in the White House.

Finally, it has to do with the times. The Reagans succeeded the Carters. In the beginning, the Carters were much admired for their relatively simple style. Jimmy Carter would go on camera sitting by the fireplace in a cardigan sweater. In the beginning of his administration that was regarded as an asset. A little later on, people began to hunger for a bit more glamour in the White House.

When Nancy Reagan first came on the scene, she was something of a culture shock. Virtually overnight, we had gone from the relatively simple peanut farmer from Georgia to a Hollywood couple. And this was perhaps too rapid a movement for the American public to take to. It was one thing to have too simple a White House. It was another thing to have a White House that appeared to us to be run more like a monarchy than a democratic republic. So for all three reasons—her own comfort with the situation, her husband's popularity, and the fact that we've now gotten used to and rather fond of a more glamorous lifestyle—she's doing much better now than she did in the beginning.

The reason First Ladies are such easy targets is that they're so exposed. The combination of being out front and associated inevitably with the policies, ideology, and attitudes of their presidential mate makes them vulnerable on multiple levels. The trick is for them to find a line between seeming to be politically appropriate and yet personally supportive. That's not easy, as we've seen, in presidents' wives and in candidates' wives.

Some, like Jacqueline Kennedy and Nancy Reagan, do feel a fairly strong need to keep themselves out of the public limelight. Some, like Lady Bird Johnson and Rosalynn Carter, however shy they may both have been to begin with—and there's ample testimony to suggest that they both began as very shy ladies—somehow overcame this and became public personas.

*The reason First Ladies are such easy targets is that they're so exposed. The combination of being out front and associated inevitably with the policies, ideology, and attitudes of their presidential mate makes them vulnerable on multiple levels.*

If you look at a book such as *Lady Bird Johnson's White House Diary*, which is a big, fat tome about her activities in the White House, you will see that there was very little time in those years that was kept to herself. Whenever she had a private minute or two, she almost wrote about it apologetically, as if she were indulging herself. Rosalynn Carter, too, was a workaholic, and most of that work life was political life.

Nancy Reagan is a more private figure than her predecessor, a more private figure than Lady Bird Johnson. But with the passage of time, we're seeing her increasingly comfortable with those moments when she is in the public eye.

Most First Ladies end up taking on the aura of their husbands. As much as we would like to say, "Let's look at the First Lady in isolation from her presidential mate," I think finally the way history will remember them, except for the few students of the subject of First Ladies, is the way their husbands are remembered. Successful presidents will tend to be accompanied in the mind's eye by successful First Ladies. The reverse is also true.

This is not to say that there are no distinctions made. Lyndon Johnson was known as a very complicated man. His presidency was in some ways very great, in others tragically flawed, while Lady Bird Johnson is almost universally admired.

If Nancy Reagan goes down in history favorably, as a good First Lady, then I think it will be in the ways that matter—she is supportive of her husband, she is appropriate in public. But finally she will be remembered in relationship to Ronald Reagan's presidency.

She understands it very well, and I think she's extremely happy.

## SHEILA TATE

*I* remember one day when there was an inconsequential story in the press. A reference attributed something happening in the West Wing to her influence. It was something she didn't even know about, didn't have any idea what they were talking about. She said, "You know, some days, I feel like if it rains, it must be my fault." And I remember thinking that she must feel so powerless sometimes to control some of these events because if someone wants to attribute something to you via an unnamed source, what can you do? She's not able to defend herself constantly. She was deeply upset about it and concerned that there should be some way to change it.

*She said, "You know, some days, I feel like if it rains, it must be my fault."*

Right: *Nancy Reagan and the Portuguese First Lady, Mrs. Eanes, in Lisbon, May 1985.*

How did she turn it around? She got on an airplane and hardly ever came back to the White House. She was on the road month after month after month. She visited treatment centers where she asked kids, "Tell me what happened? Why did this happen to you? What could you have done?" She said, "You know, you can't learn unless you listen."

She would have been on the road four months earlier had it not been for the Libyan terrorist threat, which constrained us from traveling for a while. So we went out as soon in the new year as we could. That first trip heartened her so much because she saw kids responding to her. She saw that, in just visiting one-on-one, she was having an impact, and she got so immersed in that subject that I think she forgot about herself.

If you don't set an agenda, it is set for you. If Nancy Reagan, in that first year, is meeting privately and it's not making an impact on the perceptions in the media, then, obviously, we're not setting our own agenda, even though we're doing the work.

We set our own agenda. And it was visibly done. She went out on the road. She invited the press to come with her. She took the camera that you were shining on her and turned it around and focused it on a cause—one she could do something about.

*If you don't set an agenda, it is set for you.*

*I don't think there's anything she's afraid of.*

We're talking about, probably, a thirty-point rise in the polls, what Dick Wirthlin calls a thermometer rating. Dick explained to me that it's very unusual for a known public figure to change much on that rating, more than three or four points, and hers changed twenty-five, thirty points. I think people got a better idea of who she really was, that she's an interesting, vulnerable, multi-faceted person who certainly does care about people.

I don't think there's anything she's afraid of. She still has very good judgment about herself, what she's good at and what she would shy away from and what suits her. She has a very keen focus. If some great event presented itself and I went to her and said, "I think you ought to get involved in this, what do you think?" she would know what questions to ask to assess whether it was right for her. She's always had that good sense.

I only wish that Gridiron dinner appearance had been televised. It was the most stellar moment of the single events burned in my memory. Here were six hundred publishers, major political columnists, writers in Washington, who were believing what they had been writing and reading. They thought of her as a sort of brittle, unfeeling person. There was a skit about Mrs. Reagan, making fun of her, called "Second-Hand Clothes." All of a sudden, onto the stage comes a rack of clothes—Seventh Avenue—and the clothes part and this character comes between the clothing and it's Nancy Reagan dressed in the most outrageous outfit: a skirt that didn't match, the blouse with the feather boa, a big floppy hat, and yellow rain boots, and she takes over and sings the song that, basically, makes fun of her. She was saying, "I did some really colorful things last year that you all have ribbed me about and I have a sense of humor about it. I can put it in perspective."

When I was sitting there, waiting for her to come on, it was the only time I've ever experienced what I'm sure was high blood pressure. I had these poundings in the back of my head. One publisher sitting next to me looked back at the head table and noticed that Nancy Reagan wasn't there. He leaned over to another guy and said, "Nancy Reagan isn't up there. I'll bet she's ticked."

She walked on that stage and people were so astonished, they just rose from their seats and started screaming. And when she sang this song and took this plate that represented the china and smashed it on the floor, it didn't break, so they screamed for an encore. You could feel the attitude change.

Left: *At the state dinner in San Francisco honoring Queen Elizabeth and Prince Philip, May 5, 1983.*

Right: *A private dinner for Prince Charles, held in the family quarters, May 1981.*

She stuck her neck out so far to do that. I think what got her through it was that she kept it a secret from the President. She had her clothes sent over secretly that afternoon. She went over and rehearsed very quietly. It's the only major story I know of that never got leaked in advance. Nobody knew about it except two or three people at the Gridiron and two or three people on the staff. She kept thinking, "I'm going to do this. The President's going to fall off his chair." And he darn well almost did. I think she got a lot of enjoyment out of that.

She has a very endearing, gentle sense of humor. When we first went to her, the Gridiron people suggested that she make fun of the press. She recognized right away that Nancy Reagan can't do that. She said, "I'll make fun of myself." And that turned the whole thing around.

I think a fainter heart would have shriveled up and never left the third floor of the White House. But she cared about what people thought. She never stopped caring.

I remember on a recent summer day she had three speeches in a row to groups like the P.T.A. and Lions thanking them for helping her on this big project she was involved in. It occurred to us as an afterthought, afterward, talking on the plane, that she had addressed in just ten days

*President and Mrs. Houphouët-Boigny of the Ivory Coast, at the White House, 1983.*

something like fifty thousand people. She was so self-confident, she would walk in there with a couple of cards in her hand and get up and speak extemporaneously for fifteen or twenty minutes. She had a message.

She is a woman of substance and deserves to be seen that way.

## LYN NOFZIGER

*I* suspect that Nancy has about as much as she wants to have. Nancy is not Rosalynn Carter. She doesn't view herself as the Deputy President. She doesn't want to sit in on Cabinet meetings or those sorts of things. But she certainly has a strong interest in the things that the President does. She has an interest in the people around him, and judges them on the basis of whether they serve him well. But can Nancy get someone fired? I don't think so. Ronald Reagan makes those decisions. Can Nancy get somebody hired? Probably at some levels, and maybe at some very high levels, but not totally. She's not the President, and I don't think anybody at the White House thinks she is, nor does she. There may be some people who are afraid of her, but I don't think that there's a sense of fear in the White House about Nancy. I've not seen that ever.

You take the call. Of course, you take the call. But that doesn't mean that you get on the phone and say, "Yes, Mrs. Reagan. Yes, Mrs. Reagan. Yes, Mrs. Reagan." If you take the call, then you listen. She's a very smart woman, and her opinion is worth listening to.

How much trouble are you in if she's down on you? I suspect it depends on who you are. I think you can make too much of that. I don't know of anybody, on the White House staff, on the governor's staff, who has not continued to function if Nancy was upset. The President makes the final decisions. And they're not always the decisions she thinks he ought to make. But certainly her view is taken into serious consideration, as it should be.

## ED ROLLINS

*W*hen Mrs. Reagan is concerned about something, we know that her concern always relates directly to the President. So when she's concerned about something, we respond to her, and respond to her very quickly.

*I suspect that Nancy has about as much as she wants to have.*

*I don't think anybody ever wants to be in trouble with the First Lady. She's not a petty or vindictive sort of person, but if she doesn't think that you're particularly competent, you've got to remember that she's the one who gets to talk to him first every morning and last every night.*

He's an awfully nice man, and I think that she sometimes feels that he may be a little taken advantage of by either his staff or members of the Cabinet or what have you, and she certainly wants to make sure that doesn't happen.

She certainly gets concerned about rhetoric sometimes. She's probably the one person who's always looking out for his long-term image. The two of them have made a very heavy commitment to spend a significant portion of their life here, and I think that she's very concerned about his place in history.

There's no question there've been certain members of the Cabinet she thought were becoming negative to the President and she probably weighed in pretty heavily on some of those. As far as the White House staff itself, I don't know of anyone that she's ever gone out and tried to get fired or anyone in particular that she's tried to get hired. I do believe that she has expressed opinions. There's been a time or two in which I've made statements that have caused her some concern.

I don't think anybody ever wants to be in trouble with the First Lady. She's not a petty or vindictive sort of person, but if she doesn't think that you're particularly competent, you've got to remember that she's the one who gets to talk to him first every morning and last every night. My predecessor in this job, Lyn Nofziger, and she had good periods and bad periods. The First Lady had some concerns about some of the things I've said, but certainly has backed me fully.

It's very important as the White House team moves forward with its agenda that it realize the warning signals when Mrs. Reagan is concerned about something. It's a concern that either is bothering the President or that better get some attention. When my secretary walks in and says, "Mrs. Reagan's on the line," I certainly take the call very quickly. After my heart starts beating again, I certainly listen very attentively.

## RICHARD ALLEN

*S*he makes her influence felt directly to a circle of intimates who convey her views on matters. I think that this is wholly within bounds for a First Lady. She's a strong-willed First Lady. I think good presidents are served by strong-willed ladies—that is, good assertive presidents who know where they're going, know where they've come from.

She can make her influence felt with a range of actions, from a telephone call expressing concern to perhaps making a contribution to the solution of a given problem.

*The First Lady visits young earthquake victim in Mexico City, September 1985.*

This is not a case in which a strong-willed and very capable First Lady is reaching over her husband's shoulder to try to control the ship of state. But in questions that she has an instinctive feel for, she makes her views known. I think that's utterly welcomed. My wife does it, everyone's wife does it. We find as the years accumulate that our wives gather more wisdom and their reaction becomes very important to us.

Nancy Reagan obviously has high regard for certain individuals whose fortunes she would like to push. It's only natural that she should do that. I'm sure she talks to the President about it. I've seen it in pre-White House days when she would address him very directly and begin to persuade him and then lay out a case. It was always very interesting for me to watch that. I was rather amused by it at first, and then I began to take it more seriously, not because I thought being on Nancy Reagan's good side was important. I don't believe one ought to operate that way, although there are others who may feel that this is an important operating methodology. I just went about doing my job as I saw fit. She never happened to be at cross-purposes with me. Let's say that it's infinitely preferable working for President Reagan and having Nancy Reagan on your side than having her on the other side of the street.

Without making invidious comparisons, I would say that Nancy Reagan will rate as one of the best and most effective—certainly most influential for a good cause—First Ladies in modern history.

## MICHAEL DEAVER

*Y*ou know, you sit over here in the West Wing of the White House and you start out here at six-thirty in the morning and end up at eight or nine o'clock at night, and your entire life is consumed by his schedule and the priorities of that day or the priorities of the week or the foreign visitors or the legislative schedule or whatever it is, and you forget that half a block away you've got a very integral part of what makes this man tick. Nancy is in many respects as much a part of what people think about this presidency as any First Lady in a long, long time.

I don't think she spends a lot of time on the issues. Nancy would agree with George Shultz and with Ronald Reagan and with George Bush that it's better to be talking to the Soviets than not talking to the Soviets. I think that would be her position. And I believe that's a very smart position. But it isn't the kind of thing that she would come over

*Nancy is in many respects as much a part of what people think about this presidency as any First Lady in a long, long time.*

> *She goes over
> the dotting of
> every i and
> every crossing
> of every t and
> works very hard
> to be sure that
> that's something
> that really is her
> own statement.*

here and spend a lot of time on. She might have dinner with the Shultzes or with the Bushes, and something like that might be discussed, but that's not the kind of thing she'd make a big issue of over here in the West Wing of the White House.

I think she's more confident about going out on trips and making speeches. Anybody, once they begin doing that sort of thing, develops a confidence. She takes an extraordinary amount of time in the preparation of those remarks. There's a lot of people about whom you can say, "I've got to go over to the whatchamajiggers association. Write me ten minutes, will you?" And they get it and look at it in the car on the way over. Not Nancy Reagan. She goes over the dotting of every *i* and crossing of every *t* and works very hard to be sure that that's something that really is her own statement. That's what being a First Lady is all about.

## JAMES ROSEBUSH

*I*f you can trust the polls, they say that she is respected and loved by the American people. In fact, she has a rating that indicates she's the most popular First Lady of the past seven administrations.

The people like her. She's certainly comfortable in her role. I think she sees that there's a job to be done that she can do, and she's very happy about that. She's pleased she can contribute to a major social problem, and she's seeing results on that. She's comfortable, and I think the American people are comfortable with her, too.

We know that as a result of the First Ladies coming here from seventeen different countries we're getting reports pouring in that these First Ladies are starting media campaigns to alert young people to the dangers of drug abuse. They're more knowledgeable about it. They're working with their own governments to step up efforts to cut the production of drugs. The conference was very successful.

As to those stories that Mrs. Reagan was the "star" of that big trip to Europe, when she joined her husband at the Economic Summit in Bonn, West Germany, in April and May of 1985, I think you have to take the word "star" and look at it carefully. Certainly, the President was tackling the tough issues, and he showed the kind of leadership that people were looking for from the President of the United States. She, on the other hand, had a chance to play a starring role with the people of those countries. She had a chance to get out and talk with them, and dance the flamenco with them, and show interest in their culture. In that sense, she played a starring role, but I think they starred in their own individual ways.

I don't think we've ever faced a situation where we've overshadowed the President; we've complemented him. It's exciting when she does something important—gets prominent play and people know about it. That's what we want to do. We want to communicate those things, but I don't think we've ever gotten into a situation where we've ever seriously competed with the President.

This has been the first administration in which the chief of staff to the First Lady also works for the President. I've had one foot in both wings and both their interests at heart.

I think it's a first that people in the West Wing are sitting there and saying, "Nancy Reagan is a plus. She's helping the President, politically." I expect they recognize that, so there's a degree of respect that wasn't here in previous administrations. Before, it was, "Well, let the East Wing do what they think is best. Let the First Lady get involved in charitable programs or, you know, garden parties." Which is not to denigrate what other First Ladies have done, but there's a degree of importance here, and I think it's a key point.

*I can't name a major public figure whose job rating or whose positive impressions improved as dramatically over two or three years as has Nancy Reagan's.*

# RICHARD WIRTHLIN

*R*ight from the beginning, Nancy Reagan was viewed as a dignified, strong, capable woman, but the public's perceptions have changed. That is, not only do people still articulate those as reasons why they like Nancy Reagan, but, in addition, four out of ten Americans say that they like Nancy Reagan because of her work with young people, the work she's doing fighting drugs, and her sensitivity to people.

In 1981 and 1982, she was still viewed favorably, but it wasn't as strong a feeling as it is now. About five or six out of ten said they were favorably impressed with Nancy Reagan. Those first two years in the White House were pretty rough ones for the First Lady. Since that time, she has developed a confidence and brought to her public image, if you will, a "likableness" that wasn't there early on. This plus her dedication to a cause she feels very, very deeply about made Nancy Reagan probably one of the most positively supported First Ladies in many years.

I think hers is an unusual case. It's not unusual to see

someone who has a favorable rating initially have that rating erode as time goes on. I can't name a major public figure whose job rating or whose positive impressions improved as dramatically over two or three years as has Nancy Reagan's.

## DONNIE RADCLIFFE

*S*he projected the image of a very well-to-do woman socialite who really had little concern or interest in anyone who wasn't a part of her particular social milieu. She was someone who cared about clothes and furnishings and parties and people who were her sort. The real person didn't come across at first—that she was concerned about the average person. I'm not saying she wasn't, but it never came across.

She's riding very high these days. She was very successful in Europe. She has good press. She makes no mistakes. She's very professional. She's an actress who performs her role well. She follows directions and her staff works closely

*Left: Four more years. Ronald Reagan takes the oath of office in 1985.*

*Does she enjoy all the attention? It would be very difficult for any human being not to enjoy it.*

with her. I think she's very successful right now. She's at the top.

I would like to see more specifics in her drug-abuse message. By that I mean, when she is meeting with people from other countries, if she could be more specific about what sort of things have been successful here in her own crusade.

I think she is too general; she should be more specific and say, "We did this. We had a publisher do comic books for us with a message on the dangers of drug abuse. We went to the National Pharmacists and had them start a campaign."

Does she enjoy all the attention? It would be very difficult for any human being not to enjoy it.

## WILLIAM F. BUCKLEY

*P*eople didn't go around saying Mrs. Truman was a disappointment, but Mrs. Truman was a domestic in her husband's household. She wanted really no external visage. Nancy Reagan has a background as an actress, as a performer. And it is inconceivable that she would lead so inconspicuous a life as Mrs. Truman. On the other hand, if her successor were a Mrs. Truman type, I don't think people would rush forward and say what a disappointment she is. They would simply accept the fact that the temperament of the First Lady dominates the question of how she's going to behave.

You ask, What is *her* vision of the role of First Lady, not our vision? If you accept that distinction, I would say Nancy Reagan's vision of the role of First Lady is, number one, to do everything her husband wants her to do and, number two, to identify herself publicly with the idealism and social concern of a chief of state. She simply wants to be an exemplary First Lady. The idea of what constitutes an exemplary First Lady is not set in concrete. It depends completely on the personality of the individual.

## NANCY REAGAN

*M*y meeting with the Pope was one of the most moving, wonderful experiences I've ever had. I've met with him twice before but this was the first time alone.

What was so special? Being alone. Talking about something that concerns me very much and concerns him, and hearing his views on it—and his comments about what I'm doing.

Yes, he thought what we're doing is important. You can't ask for anything more. How could you not be moved?

We discussed the seriousness of the drug problem. I believe very strongly in the family, getting parents' groups and families involved. He believes just as strongly that it's necessary for these young people who are trying to work their way back—which is a very difficult thing for them to do—to have some kind of spiritual help, religious help.

He's such a marvelous man. Number one, a very strong man, but he has a gentleness at the same time. The attempted assassinations came very closely together, so I feel a special affinity with him.

*My meeting with the Pope was one of the most moving, wonderful experiences I've ever had.*

*I just hope whatever I say or do can be of help to people. It's special to be here on my own, but on those terms—only on those terms.*

I just hope whatever I say or do can be of help to people. It's special to be here on my own, but on those terms—only on those terms. That I can be of help.

## RON REAGAN

*I*'ve never sat down and tried to rate First Ladies. I'd say that, in terms of what she's done for the White House, she'd have to be way up there at the top. The place was a mess when she got there, really a mess. It looked, you know, real low rent, kind of Holiday Inn—as much as the White House can look like a Holiday Inn. She's really fixed it up. She took a beating because of the china. Well, nobody talked about the fact that they didn't have a whole set of china any more. The last person, I think, who actually bought a set for the White House was Lady Bird—maybe it goes back to Jackie Kennedy. When they have state dinners there, people swipe plates and stuff. Little plates disappear into handbags and coat pockets, so they couldn't have a dinner and have a complete setting of china for everybody. She thought it was kind of tacky, so she went out and got some of her friends to donate the money for it.

Eleanor Roosevelt is kind of an icon now. She's really "big time." As far as Jackie and Lady Bird go, in terms of

style, I'd rate my mother with them, sure. If Jackie had come along when my mother did, when society wasn't quite amenable to a stylish First Lady, she'd have gotten a beating, too. You know, my mom can dress with the best of 'em—even Jackie. And she has beautified the White House. There's no question about that.

## MAUREEN REAGAN

*B*efore they came to Washington, she always had a good deal of control over their lives, over how they spent their time. All of a sudden, she came into a house that wasn't hers, trying to make it into the home she wanted it to be. She was suddenly giving dinner parties and luncheons that she had not been there to plan, that were suddenly thrust upon her. I talked to her one day about two weeks after the inauguration and I said, "Well, how is it going?" And she said, "Well, it's okay. I'm giving my fourth luncheon tomorrow afternoon and they didn't tell me till twenty minutes ago."

Well, you can't be an expert at giving state dinners till you've given two or three of them; but once you have, if you learn from what goes on, and you learn the mix of people and what makes them a good event, a good state event, then you say, "Well, good, now I can do that, so now I don't have to worry about the state dinner that's going to be held in April because I know these are the things that work." In other words, you can't be an expert on living in the White House until you've lived in the White House for a while.

Everything she has done has given her another level of confidence. Instead of going back and starting at "A" every time, she has gone from "A" to "B" to "C" to "D" to "E" to "F," until now she's up around "X," "Y," and "Z."

The job of the First Lady of the United States is being the ultimate corporate wife, and I am not a big fan of the whole system that creates this corporate structure in which we have these non-paid people on whom we depend to do much of the work that goes on. It seems to me that there should be a salary for the First Lady of the United States, because certainly it's somebody who is on call twenty-four hours a day, seven days a week, doing a lot of jobs that most of us wouldn't want to do.

There is a definition of a First Lady. It would be the same if it was a First Gentleman. There is a job description. The First Spouse of the United States has the responsibility

*Well, you can't be an expert at giving state dinners till you've given two or three of them; but once you have, you learn from what goes on, and you learn the mix of people and what makes them a good event.*

*And it's a job that has to be dealt with every day. It's something people have to understand— that the house doesn't just run by itself.*

for the residence of the White House, for the social events, for the tours, for all that comes under that particular bailiwick. That is a massive corporation to be running, and that alone—without the social functions, without looking for the thing that you want to use your office to help people with, without the fact that you also have a family, and that you have brought your own way of life with you to the White House—is a massive job. And it's a job that has to be dealt with every day. It's something people have to understand— that house doesn't just run by itself.

The First Lady of the United States is a powerful woman. She's obviously got an awful lot of influence over what goes on in her domain, which is that house, though I don't know how that translates into policy decisions.

If I have ideas on programs that I'm going to present, as part of what I do, to the chairman of the Republican National Committee, I sit and talk to my husband over dinner, and I say, "I'm thinking of doing this," and he says, "Well, listen, why don't you take that and go one step further, or why don't you back up and move in that direction, and if you consolidated this particular plan, you wouldn't use as much effort and you'd get much more progress on it," and I get all this refined. Now I take my plan in and everybody thinks I'm brilliant, because I've got this other brilliant person to come along and help me.

Well, the President doesn't just sit there and wait for people to bring him things. He has ideas. He sees things unfolding. He reads. He gathers ideas. So he goes into a meeting of the economic advisers and he's got an idea about something. Well, he's not going to just throw it out there. No human being would do that. He might sit at dinner the night before and say, "I was reading about this and thinking about this and I was thinking we can move in this direction." And she says, "Well, that's kind of interesting. Yeah, that sounds good to me. But wait a minute. What if you did such-and-such?" And so he goes down the next day and it all gets into the mix and everybody gets into it, so it's not her idea. It's not her influencing policy, but it's his sounding-board. He has to refine his thinking before he goes into the melee and make it all come together.

But it's like playing telephone when you're a kid. I say it to you, somebody else hears it, and the next thing you know, you have the *National Enquirer* writing a piece called "Nancy Reagan Creates White House Policy." She doesn't need that. The President doesn't need that. It's not good for the political dynamics of the country. So she's very uncomfortable, because she's afraid that people will not listen to what it is indeed that she does do.

I did not know Eleanor Roosevelt. Unfortunately, she

was just a wee tad before my time. The first First Lady that I can remember knowing anything about was Bess Truman. I've known about Bess Truman and Mamie Eisenhower and Jackie Kennedy and Lady Bird Johnson and Pat Nixon and Betty Ford and Rosalynn Carter and Nancy Reagan. That's eight. She's the best.

*A morning meeting in the First Lady's chief of staff's office.*

# 5

# *The Nancy Reagan Style*

## NANCY REAGAN

*I* want more pomp, though I'm not going to criticize any other administration. I think the White House and any function that takes place at the White House should have a certain sense of dignity about it. I think the public wants it. I don't believe the public wants a man to just walk into the room. They want to know that it's the President.

Do I like "Hail to the Chief"? Yes. It's traditional. It's always been traditional and I think it's important to keep that tradition up. After all, this is a very special place. I keep saying that, but it is. The White House is where all of our history emanated from. All of our presidents, everything happened right here where we are. When you look out the window at the Washington Monument and the Jefferson Memorial, it's a wonderful feeling.

I was unprepared for the condition of the second and third floors. I didn't realize they hadn't really been tended to, maintained. They hadn't been painted in something like fifteen or twenty years. The floors hadn't been done. All the varnish was peeling off the wooden doors. And this, after all, is the White House, which should look right.

*After all, this is a very special place.*

*We had a party for my husband's birthday and I wore a dress that I've had for twelve years. The one I wore to Mrs. Thatcher's dinner I've had for fifteen years.*

Below: *A White House dinner for Chancellor Helmut Schmidt of Germany, May 1981.*

Right: *Dancing at the second inaugural, 1985.*

I do not spend that much money on clothes. I do not buy that many clothes. What clothes I buy, I wear forever. My husband teases me and says I still have my gym bloomers from school.

It's not true about spending twenty-five thousand dollars on a wardrobe. Now we get back to all the other First Ladies who have had the exact same problem. I don't know why it always happens, since it's not true at all. I never paid sixteen hundred dollars for any kind of a handbag. That's just untrue.

If I were spending that kind of money, I would think people would have a right to say, What in the world is she doing? But I'm not. I suppose there's a point at which, if it's yours and you want to spend it the way you want to, spend it, but I just would never spend that kind of money on my clothes. They were very wrong about a handbag or whatever. Anybody can say anything they want to say and you have no recourse, really.

We had a party for my husband's birthday and I wore a dress that I've had for twelve years. The one I wore to Mrs. Thatcher's dinner I've had for fifteen years.

## LETITIA BALDRIDGE

*S*he received a lot of flak for buying beautiful clothes and looking so wonderful. There was so much interest in the designers of her clothes, she was made absolutely furious and for a while had only one designer, Oleg Cassini, do everything just to keep away all the press interest. It used to be that way in all administrations, a very fashionable First Lady. I'm sure it was true in Dolley Madison's day— the whole world could be falling apart but still the questions would be coming into the White House, What is she going to wear and who made that dress?

The public would be very sad and very disappointed if our First Lady were dowdy and badly dressed. She does represent American fashion. She does look like a million dollars. As a matter of fact, all of our First Ladies have looked like a million dollars recently. We've been very lucky, and that helps the American fashion industry.

There was a lot of flak about Mrs. Kennedy's clothes. That finally disappeared, as it has with Mrs. Reagan.

They both share an equal sense of style, an equal ease at entertaining, a wonderful sense of rightness. When Mrs. Kennedy came into the White House, it was in terrible shape, and she put it into good shape, thanks to the Fine Arts Committee. Every First Lady thereafter added to the

*The public would be very sad and very disappointed if our First Lady were dowdy and badly dressed.*

Above: *Princess Grace and Mrs. Reagan meet for dinner while in London for the wedding of Prince Charles, July 1981.*

Below: *The President and First Lady welcome Princess Caroline and Prince Albert of Monaco to the White House, May 28, 1983.*

White House and made it better and better, as has Mrs. Reagan. It's been an evolution of style in that house—acquisitions of beautiful historic items and things of beauty in that house. It used to look like a bargain basement on sale day. Now it looks great.

It's fascinating to look at the First Ladies we've had. When you look back in history, the ones who emerge are Abigail Adams, who was sort of a feminist, and Dolley Madison, who was criticized for her beautiful clothes from Paris. James Madison was roundly criticized in the press for bringing back the Vermeil service of flatware—the forks, knives, and spoons that are used at some of the state dinner functions.

What is sad to see is that the great Vermeil flatware service is subtracted from every year as White House guests pocket forks, knives, and spoons to take home as souvenirs. They're taking priceless museum treasures out of the White House, but they don't seem to mind.

## DR. BARBARA KELLERMAN

*W*hen she first entered the White House, there was a tremendous tendency to jump on her for her attention to clothes, to china in the White House, to what was considered frivolous, trivial, and somehow not worthy of the contemporary American woman. Nancy Reagan held up with good grace under those early attacks. Women in general are dressing up more than they did in the sixties and seventies. There is a new attention to manners. There's a new attention to propriety.

Jacqueline Kennedy spent a lot of money. When one looks at First Ladies, one really needs to look at them in the context of the entire presidential family and the political impact of the presidential family in their day and age.

## RON REAGAN

*M*ost movie people are fairly well off. I think it's unreasonable to think she's going to go out and hang out at truck stops or something. Most of their friends are pretty well off. That's just the way it is.

I don't see her as nouveau riche, in terms of sensibilities, at least. In her present position, it's important for her to put the presidency and the White House in as good a light as she can, and she wants everything to be right. She wants everything to be first class.

## MARY JANE WICK

*N*ancy is a very gracious person, and a person with exquisite taste. She always has had that. She's a very private person and sometimes can be shy. Her friends are involved in the community and have lived very full lives. Nancy looks lovely in whatever she's wearing. She also looks marvelous in blue jeans and tennis shoes up at the ranch.

## WILLIAM F. BUCKLEY

*I*t has been suggested that the Buckleys and Jerry Zipkin and Brooke Astor represent a kind of New York society crowd that she wants to be accepted by. What do I think of that? Well, I don't think the First Lady has difficulty being accepted in any crowd. At a social level, she's pretty much at the head of the table wherever she goes. I think she gravitates to certain people for reasons obvious, some of them eccentric. Jerry Zipkin is a very unusual human being and she is devoted to him. Brooke Astor she didn't know much before the President was elected. She's known us for twenty-five years. So there's a sort of mix there.

The First Lady has no problems of that sort. I suppose if she decides that she wanted to be accepted by the fellows at All Souls College in Oxford, she'd have certain problems. But the kind of life she has, she has no difficulty whatever in making out.

## BILL BLASS

*I*'ve made clothes for Nancy Reagan for years. There is something special about the lady in that she literally cannot look bad in anything. It's amazing because she's small and, in theory, we make clothes for mannequins that are quite tall. Yet she can really adapt almost any style to her own particular way of wearing clothes. She's an extremely easy gal to dress.

She's also extremely easy to work with because she has very definite ideas about what she looks well in and what is

*In her present position, it's important for her to put the presidency and the White House in as good a light as she can, and she wants everything to be right. She wants everything to be first class.*

Right: *With Mary Martin at a fundraising gala.*

Above: *The First Lady and Charlton Heston in the family quarters.*

appropriate to her role as First Lady. That's her total awareness of the role she's playing. This applies to daytime as well as evening.

I suspect that Mrs. Reagan is not really a trend setter in the sense we in fashion relate to it. What she does is adopt the best from several designers. She wears clothes for her own way of life and for what is becoming to her. She has a marvelous awareness of what is appropriate for her as First Lady.

I think Nancy Reagan already has had a tremendous impact on fashion in that she has a sureness of taste that relates to a great many women across the country. Pretty clothes, feminine clothes—she obviously dresses to please the President. Therefore, a lot of women follow suit and dress to please men. Chauvinistic remark, I know.

Nancy Reagan also has had an effect on people's appreciation not only of fashion but of entertaining and running a house. She takes a vital interest in not just clothes but in running a very beautiful house, one of the most beautiful houses in the world, and doing it superbly.

How often do I design something for Nancy Reagan? We send her videos of the shows. Obviously, she can't come to the shows herself and, seasonally, maybe twice a year, we plan things that she needs. It's not done on any planned basis. It just depends entirely on her travel plans, entertainment plans, her public plans. We'll talk on the phone about it. If I'm in Washington, I'll go over and lunch with her and we'll discuss it then.

It certainly isn't at all evident that she's demanding in the role we play together as one of her designers. The special-occasion dresses that I best remember I made for her are the

*There is something special about the lady in that she literally cannot look bad in anything.*

ones she wore to the galas preceding the inaugurations. The first time she was in black, which we thought was appropriate because she was not going to wear black for any of the other ceremonies. The second time she wore red. As you know, she loves red. But I'm always amazed. She'll drag out a dress that's five or six years old, even older, and wear it.

She is partial, of course, to certain styles and colors. And I think she very wisely chooses red, white, and black very often. She's amazingly good at colors. Strange colors, an odd shade of green or something of that sort, she looks well in. But she does rather restrict it to black, white, and red.

Without really being conscious of it, I must have made clothes for her under a different label than I have now. Even before she was the First Lady of California, she had purchased clothes of mine. I've seen, of course, a great deal of concern on her part, not only for her husband but for the nation, which is perfectly obvious. It's very difficult for me to judge whether she seems more assertive or ambitious because she has never seemed that way to me and she doesn't seem that way now. She's sure of herself, which is a damned important thing to be.

It's always very difficult to make comparisons between a First Lady and any of the First Ladies who preceded her. I suspect that since Mrs. Onassis, there has been no one who's had an impact in fashion as much as Mrs. Reagan. But that's because she has always dressed well and has always been interested in clothes, just as Mrs. Onassis was, too.

I suspect quite honestly that the things she's happiest in are the things she wears in Santa Barbara on the ranch. Obviously, jeans and a cotton shirt are her favorite.

Of course, she enjoys dressing up. But show me a woman who doesn't. There are special occasions, special times, when any gal wants to look great. She's not an exception.

I think one of the things that Nancy Reagan has tried to emphasize from the first is that the role of First Lady does demand a certain dignity and a certain style, not only in dressing but in attitude. She's a master at that. She's, well, representing our nation. And for that, I think, bravo for looking well.

# 6

## *Nancy and Controversy*

### NANCY REAGAN

$\mathcal{A}$s I look back on it, I'm sure I'd probably do things differently.

Since no money came from the taxpayers, nothing seemed wrong to me about redoing the White House. Nothing had been done on the third floor in thirty years. There were cracks in the walls. It needed painting. It needed maintenance. It needed furniture taken out of storage. I'm a nester, I like to fix things up. But nothing was being taken out of the taxpayers' pocket, so it didn't seem wrong. The china was donated to the White House. I didn't buy china. The people who donated the china have often thought of it. They never got the credit they really were due.

We've tightened our belts in many ways. We're not spending as much money. We're just pulling in. You have to.

Was the 1982 Gridiron dinner the turning point? Yes. I remember being scared to death. My husband didn't know anything about it. We had rehearsed up here without his knowing anything about it. We had two rehearsals, as I remember. The outfit was unbelievable. It was every crazy thing you could possibly think of, rubber boots, mangy. It

*As I look back on it, I'm sure I'd probably do things differently.*

Above: *Representing the United States at the International First Ladies' Briefing on Drugs in April 1985. The First Ladies of seventeen nations attended.*

was something. At the end of the dinner, while the entertainment was going on, I excused myself from the table and went backstage to change. I'm sure he must have thought, "Where in the world is she? She's been gone for such a long time." And when I came out, I was scared. But then it seemed to go well, and I thought to myself, "I hope he thinks it's going well."

I'd hoped to blunt all of this stuff that had been said that was not me, to put it more in perspective and get people back on the right track. They applauded.

I have opinions of different people. If I feel they're hurting my husband, or if I feel that they're trying to end-run him or use him or whatever, then I'll say something.

I never asked the Carters to move out. I mean, never! How would I? Never. The only thing that I can think of is that we were at dinner, during the inauguration. We started from Blair House, as is customary. During the actual swearing in, the White House staff moves the First Family—the Carters, in this case—out of the White House and us in. And I was saying, "I don't know how they do it. It must be a tremendous task to perform in a few hours." Everybody was agreeing and I just said that I really don't know how they do it. Maybe a good idea would be for us, when we move out, to move into Blair House and make it a little bit easier.

The "tiny little gun" that was written about disappeared quite a long time ago. I had the tiny little gun when my husband was away a great deal of the time and I was alone. I was advised to have it.

Am I fudging two years in age? I might. I haven't made up my mind yet. That's a pretty good answer, isn't it? In Hollywood, you were never over twenty-five. At least I progressed beyond twenty-five.

## BETTY FRIEDAN

*U*nfortunately, I do not think that Nancy Reagan has done anything to advance the cause of women, which is a very pointed fault or bad mark against her, regardless of specific politics—Republican, Democrat. Women in the last twenty years have made this great breakthrough in America. We broke through the feminine mystique. We said, "We are people." We fought for the personhood of women, and the control of our own lives, our own voice. We demanded and fought for equal opportunity. We aren't finished yet, and there's even a backlash against it.

We were at college together, at Smith. I was editor of the paper and literary magazine and she was an actress. She had the spirit to go to Broadway, to go to Hollywood. As I said to her when I went on the press bus at several conventions before she actually became First Lady, "Nancy, you are a Smith person, and how can you not be for equal rights for women? You were one of the career women before it was even popular." And she said, "Oh, well, I'm for equal treatment, and so is Ronnie, and I'm for rights, but I'm not for the amendment."

Well, that's just specious. When he was elected President and she became First Lady, I went up to her at the Gridiron dinner and I shook her hand and I said, "Use your power. Be a good role model now for women, and use your power to keep the door open, or open it wide for women."

*If I feel they're hurting my husband, or if I feel that they're trying to end-run him or use him or whatever, then I'll say something.*

*She's not a star in the soap opera, she is the First Lady. And we expect in America that our First lady somehow embody the values of where women are at this time.*

It just seems to me that's her obligation as a woman of her generation, at this time in history, and she hasn't done it. She has not raised her voice. They say she is now one of the most powerful influences in the Reagan Administration or on the President. Why has she not tried to stop him from this war on the right of women to control their own bodies and the safe, legal, medical access to abortion? Why has she not tried to stop him when the Reagan Administration has given the word that the laws now on the books on sex discrimination in employment and education shouldn't be enforced, or that affirmative action should now be used to restore the supremacy of the white male?

She's not a star in the soap opera, she is the First Lady. And we expect in America that our First Lady somehow embody the values of where women are at this time. When you think, fifty years ago, of Eleanor Roosevelt, you realize what a role model she would still be, even today. You think of Betty Ford—who really was gutsy, not only in behalf of equal rights for women but very honest on the question of abortion and what she would do about her own daughter if there were such a need—being brutally honest about her own problems with alcoholism and so on. She was a fine role model.

Breathes there a woman with a soul so dead, an educated woman in the eighties that cannot identify with this great liberation of women to be people? Maybe deep down, she does. Maybe that's what this supposed new change in image is all about. Maybe she just, somehow, has to be a person, and that's why she's moving more, being more serious about matters like drug abuse.

I'm not that much of an expert on the life and personal history of Nancy Reagan, but I do recall that her own stepfather was arch-conservative, arch-reactionary, and she might have had a reactionary influence on Ronald Reagan politically.

She was a career woman before it was fashionable, when most of our classmates were in condominiums, making a career out of marriage and four children and baking their own bread. She went to Hollywood and she went to Broadway, but now, as First Lady, she is an anachronism. She is somehow not only denying her earlier reality but the reality of American women today—what they want to be and what they need to be and what I think they would like represented in the First Lady, who should represent the highest standards and values for women, Republican and Democrat.

There is an expectation today that a woman can be and should be all the person she is capable of being. She wants and values the choice to have children. She will be her husband's wife if she chooses to marry. But she will be a person, seriously committed to her own voice in society. We are not

*Nancy, you are a Smith person, and
how can you not be for
equal rights for women? You were one
of the career women before
it was even popular.*

finished yet in this great massive revolution of women to full personhood and full equality. So I say to Nancy Reagan, "Why have you not used your role in the White House to give a fuller role model for younger women?"

I wouldn't fault her if she's not the same kind of feminist I am. She doesn't have to be a card-carrying NOW member. Nobody would expect that of a Republican woman. But Betty Ford, who's a Republican, was courageous and outspoken on behalf of the basic move of women to equality. Here, Nancy Reagan, whose husband's administration is mounting a backlash against women's rights, is not raising her voice against it. Have her advisers told her, "Look, American women really didn't vote for your husband in numbers"?

The Madame Chiang Kai-shek role—that's where her press has been lately, that she is propping him up or manipulating him or controlling him. If that is so, so be it. American woman have a great hunger for more power. They have been too powerless, and they'll get it whatever way they can. If you're lucky enough to be First Lady, you should use that role for all it's worth. For good things.

I remember in the turbulent days of China, it came out that Madame Chiang Kai-shek, who was Wellesley-educated,

*We are not finished yet in this great massive revolution of women to full personhood and full equality. So I say to Nancy Reagan, "Why have you not used your role in the White House to give a fuller role model for younger women?"*

I believe, was sort of like a Dragon Lady. She really was pulling the strings. It's coming out that Nancy Reagan is one of the most influential people in the administration. Well, then, in what direction is this influence going?

I don't think anybody would have criticized Nancy Reagan forty years ago for just being a clothes horse, for the china that she is buying, or whether she's wearing the clothes of this designer or that designer. Even now, as a feminist, I am interested in fashion and I think women are still interested in fashion. She can be as fashionable as she pleases. But there's got to be something more than that. I mean, Eleanor Roosevelt was a giant among women. We don't have that kind of image of Mrs. Eisenhower, but that was in the fifties when the whole country was pulling back from the American adventure.

Lady Bird Johnson—there was quite a woman there. Jacqueline Kennedy—everybody went ga-ga over her fashion and her decorative style, but there was a mind there that brought poetry and art to the White House. I remember thinking at the time, if she would only stop using that whispery voice. You wanted her to be more.

Betty Ford was a very interesting example of a woman who started out in a very conventional way but lived up to the demands and the expectation of women. Is there something really going to emerge in Nancy Reagan where she senses that she could use her power on issues today where women's futures are in jeopardy?

## DR. BARBARA KELLERMAN

*T*he position of the Reagan Administration on women's issues such as abortion and the Equal Rights Amendment has been somewhat hard to determine. They have had a house feminist in that family, but it has not really been Nancy, but the President's eldest daughter, Maureen Reagan.

This has been very carefully done. It was more articulated in the '84 campaign than in '80. Nancy Reagan's role with regard to equal rights and abortion has been relatively quiescent. Intermittently, she has given slightly mixed signals on the subject, but she is a far cry from her two predecessors, Betty Ford and Rosalynn Carter, who both came out very strongly for the Equal Rights Amendment. In that sense, if you are a feminist, if you believe in the Equal Rights Amendment, you would see the Reagan Administration, and Nancy Reagan in particular, as a step back.

## NANCY REYNOLDS

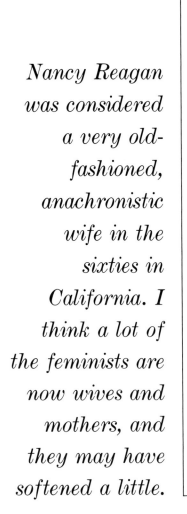

*Nancy Reagan was considered a very old-fashioned, anachronistic wife in the sixties in California. I think a lot of the feminists are now wives and mothers, and they may have softened a little.*

*N*ancy Reagan was considered a very old-fashioned, anachronistic wife in the sixties in California. I think a lot of the feminists are now wives and mothers, and they may have softened a little. Nancy Reagan hasn't changed, basically. But you know, she's always felt that people should do what they have to do and she would hope that people would respect how she feels.

Isn't it interesting that so many feminists today are saying, "Look, it's fine if women don't want to work and stay home for kids." That's okay. But it has taken the feminists—and I'm a feminist—a long time to come around to saying there is a lot to be said for women who have no interest in a career and who feel that their career is their family and their husbands, when they can financially manage to make it that full time.

So I think that it has moved toward the other side a little. Nancy Reagan hasn't personally changed at all. After all, she has two very feminist daughters and she was like all

of us with our children during the sixties. We had a lot of confrontations and Nancy Reagan stuck by her guns about how she felt about things. I bet if you interview the children, you will find that they have mellowed a great deal.

# RICHARD ALLEN

*I* would say that the President has a tendency not to be engaged in staff difficulties and dustups. And hers is not the opposite tendency to get involved, but certainly she's not reluctant to voice her views.

I think she addresses the unpleasant tasks, though ultimately the decisions are his and he must take the responsibility for them.

She played no role at all in the political infighting. There was a decided campaign to have Haig and me engage. Al Haig and I have analyzed this. There wasn't nearly as much substance to the fabled Allen–Haig battles as has met the eye. There was a very well-orchestrated campaign by colleagues in the White House to make it appear that we were constantly embattled.

Al has a steel-spring personality, and I'm not reluctant to engage, from time to time, on issues or even on procedures. But this was exacerbated deliberately by some individuals in the White House. And I think the reflection of that as it played in the newspaper came back to Mrs. Reagan.

Obviously, she couldn't be happy about discord and disharmony in the administration under any circumstances. On top of that, we had an administration that was trying to devote its exclusive attention to domestic affairs for the first year. The Secretary of State, Al, wanted foreign policy issues to get a share of attention. I shared the President's agenda in trying to keep foreign policy—national security— not inconsequential but on a low key, on the back burner. And that led to further misunderstandings. Nancy Reagan, I think, was influential, but it wasn't because she came to all of the judgments that she made by herself unassisted. She didn't do that unaided.

I think it was very clear at the time, while I was on a leave of absence and the canard and innuendo that surrounded my case were being investigated by the Department of Justice—there were messages that I should resign, and my answer was that I certainly would not resign until I knew what the outcome would be. Until such time, I wouldn't address the question of my future—until such time as I was cleared, as I knew, inevitably, I would be cleared.

Then I was repeatedly cleared of these really trumped-up innuendos and allegations. I gather that, at one point, she joined some colleagues in the White House apart from those who were defending me and thought it would be best if I left.

But I wouldn't do it. My reputation was at stake, my family, my future, my integrity, my character. And until that was cleared, there wasn't anything that would cause me to leave.

I have no tangible evidence of her role except what I would read in the newspapers. Now, Nancy Reagan was not talking to newspapers, but there were those in her circle who were. And you couldn't distinguish between them. This is part of the problem in Washington, the great anonymous source.

I maintained a cordial relationship with Nancy Reagan in the years after my departure from the White House. I see her from time to time, talk to her, and there isn't the slightest hint of bitterness or anything else. I happen to support the President's agenda. I don't support people, I support ideas. I think she and the President know that. Perhaps that has led to a more understanding relationship between us.

## MICHAEL DEAVER

*N*one of us really realized the public scrutiny or the media scrutiny that would be put on every little thing we did and said. There were some nasty articles. I don't think it was really a lot of anti-Nancy personal press like there was in California. I don't think there's been that here, really.

Some of those people basically disagreed with her husband's philosophy. And so they might have used her to get back at Ronald Reagan and what his policies represented.

Nancy is a very direct person. She is not one who likes to sit around and brood about an issue. She'd just as soon get it on the table.

## LYN NOFZIGER

*A*ll the criticism of her fixing up the living quarters was just outrageous because, one, she didn't use tax money, and two, the living quarters hadn't been fixed up in years. The floors, for instance, had not been done since

*None of us really realized the public security or the media scrutiny that would be put on every little thing we did and said.*

Harry Truman's time. To jump on her for that, for the new dishes that were contributed by a foundation, it just seemed to me that there were people out there looking to get her.

*A meeting of the White House Conference on Drug Abuse and Families, March 1982.*

## STUART SPENCER

She was, to a degree, insecure, and you could see it. The media could see it, definitely. But I have another theory. Ronald Reagan came in with a mandate. Ronald Reagan was hot property. Ronald Reagan had a lot of successes, and when you look at Washington, you look at the system we have here, where you have the government and the press and they're in basically adversarial positions. There was no way the media could get at Ronald Reagan. He wasn't vulnerable; he was very successful. My theory is that the media decided that every day can't be puff-piece day, and a job was done on Nancy Reagan. She was more vulnerable.

She wasn't prepared for that sort of thing. She was in a state of shock. Being governor of California is a wonderful thing, but it's the minor leagues compared to the presidency of the United States. The capital press in Sacramento is not the capital press in Washington.

## RICHARD WIRTHLIN

*W*hen Nancy Reagan first came into the White House, there was a spate of stories that highlighted her spending. Republicans, whether they're coming into the White House in 1980 or 1972 or in the fifties, are always viewed as the party of the more wealthy and affluent.

The press took the china issue and made it symbolic—this would be a regal presidency. They used Nancy Reagan very much as that symbol. When we asked people what they liked and disliked about Nancy, her perceived penchant for liking expensive surroundings was much more prominent than it is today.

The attack had a chilling effect on Nancy. She tended to retreat, to be more defensive, to be more guarded. That provided in itself some reinforcement perhaps, at least perceptually, for some of the charges that were made.

But she's a tough, strong person. She was not at all happy or satisfied with the way she was being portrayed. She recognized that she could help both the President and a lot of other people by taking a more active or a more public role on some things that she'd always felt very concerned about.

The perception that she was somewhat snobbish, that she was aloof, that she was more interested in putting on a state dinner than anything else, that she was pushing for expensive china was much more dominant, and, I think, was clearly a bum rap. But there were reasons, far beyond Nancy Reagan, for those impressions to be reinforced.

Queen Nancy was the image that was being portrayed. She took the charge of being Queen Nancy and said, "How ridiculous." She borrowed a page from the President's book and used humor to defuse the charges: "I would never be anointed. It would mess up my hair." She had the ability and the grace under pressure, if you will, to rise above those kinds of charges.

## DONNIE RADCLIFFE

*L*ittle things that might not have seemed so important or monumental when he was governor, they felt were blown out of proportion. I think there were several things, several ways in which they got off to a bad start. One of them, before he even became President, was a flurry over the choice of her press secretary. Mrs. Reagan also made some unthinking remarks about having a gun at her bedside

*On the road with the anti-drug campaign.*

Right: *Presenting the National Teacher of the Year Award, April 1981.*

table. There were reports that the Reagans wanted the Carters out of the White House so that they could do the redecorating. Whether or not any of that was true, it started them off on the wrong foot.

The problem was that people felt that Mrs. Reagan was not concerned about what the problems of the day were, the economic hardships of certain groups in this country. For a lavish decorating program to be undertaken almost immediately after the Reagans entered the White House seemed so frivolous. I don't think their friends helped them very much.

There's a popular view that there has to be a lightning rod for Ronald. Sorry. I know that's a popular view and I think it really isn't an accurate one. I think she generated those stories and those opinions by her own actions and her own attitudes.

Ronald Reagan did come in as an extremely popular man. He came in to establishment Washington and immediately was acceptable, something Jimmy Carter was not. But in Nancy Reagan's case, I don't really understand the thinking that has her taking the flak for things that couldn't be said about him. It just doesn't make any sense.

## BONITA GRANVILLE WRATHER

*I* think the criticism of her lifestyle is erroneous. She's always been a lady who is well dressed, has grace and style, and she brings that to the White House. And that's very important. After all, we have all the other countries in the world looking at us.

## LETITIA BALDRIDGE

*S*he was the governor's wife. I've watched people who have been very big fishes in the small ponds that are their home towns deal with the press. There's nothing like the White House. Everything changes. Every single movement you make, every flick of an eyelash, is scrutinized. It is the classic goldfish bowl. I remember in the Kennedy years, Mrs. Kennedy used to devise every route possible to get out of the White House grounds without being seen by the press and the public.

*She's always been a lady who is well dressed, has grace and style, and she brings that to the White House.*

*What do I say to the Betty Friedans and other feminists who criticize? I suggest that they go back and read their own books.*

## SHEILA TATE

It was the day ketchup was declared a vegetable for school lunch programs that the White House china story broke. I haven't thought the same of ketchup since.

## MAUREEN REAGAN

I've always told her that if she was married to anybody in the world but Ronald Reagan, she would not be against the Equal Rights Amendment. Nancy Reynolds and I told her that years ago, back in the seventies. You have to understand. Here's a woman in this particular relationship who has had all of the freedom that you can have to make all of the choices. I just feel that if she had not had that kind of freedom, perhaps she would be out on the street marching with the rest of us.

What do I say to the Betty Friedans and other feminists who criticize? I suggest that they go back and read their own books.

# 7

## The First Lady's Causes

### NANCY REAGAN

*D*rug abuse is a very serious problem—among youth, among working people. It's the most democratic problem that I know of. It crosses all lines. There are no social, economic, political, or color lines. It crosses everything.

I feel very strongly about marijuana. I think it's a good deal more harmful than most children realize. I've been to Day Top Village in New York a few times, which is doing a wonderful job. All those young people in there started on marijuana. I asked them if they were for the legalization of marijuana. Every one of them said no, which is interesting. I didn't really expect them to say no.

When it first started out in the sixties, this was all a brand-new thing, and a frightening thing. Nobody knew quite how to handle it, and they were embarrassed. They thought their child was the only child on drugs. And some of them were too busy with their own lives and didn't get involved with their children's lives. They weren't wise enough to notice the little tell-tale signs. As we've progressed more into the seventies and eighties, we're more aware. Parents are more aware, more scared, as well they should be.

You can't be pessimistic about anything. You always have to be optimistic that you can solve something, anything

in life. I think the fact that these parents' groups have sprung up voluntarily, all over, is a great sign that parents are getting involved, are becoming more knowledgeable. They're not only becoming more knowledgeable, but it brings their families closer together. There's been a tendency for families to split apart. Now they're pulling together.

The drug program can sustain itself. It hasn't been cut off from all funds. It has funds, but the most important thing is that parents and corporations, business people, all become involved, all know what's happening to the people who are working for them, or their children, and do something about it.

Am I really committed to this issue? Of course I am. Because it's so dangerous. Because we do stand a chance of losing a whole generation to drugs. It's a very, very dangerous problem we're all facing.

It's not just our country that has this problem. On almost every state visit at the White House I will have coffee with other First Ladies and they always bring up the drug

*You can't be pessimistic about anything. You always have to be optimistic that you can solve something, anything in life.*

*Nobody wanted me to do it, the drug issue. I guess they thought it was kind of a downer. It's not a cheery subject. But I think I've brought it to a level of awareness that wasn't there before.*

problem. At first I thought, maybe, it was just because they knew I was interested in the drug situation, but then it became obvious that they were aware that this was happening in their own countries. They wanted to know. They were asking for advice. So that was the next logical step. If you could catch it right at the beginning, then, maybe, you could do a lot of good.

I hope I made them aware of the whole global aspect of this and gave them some suggestions and ideas. We've been at it longer than many have and I hope I was able to help.

Nobody wanted me to do it, the drug issue. I guess they thought it was kind of a downer. It's not a cheery subject. But I think I've brought to it a level of awareness that wasn't there before. I hope more people are aware of how bad the drug problem is and how widespread it is and how dangerous it is. I don't see as many comedians, now, making jokes about it, thank goodness. It's not a funny thing. I see more programs on television about it, hear more people coming forward and talking about what it's done to their lives, to their relationships, to their jobs.

It's my understanding that there was no money cut. There was money given to the states in block grants, but money was not cut. That's number one. Number two, I don't believe with any problem that money is the whole answer. Money doesn't buy love or affection or attention or involvement, all those things that have to be there. Only people provide those things, and, particularly, parents.

## BARBARA KELLERMAN

*I*t's volunteer work of a particular kind. It tends to fall into categories that, for lack of a better word, I would describe as being of a feminine nature. They have to do with health. They have to do with beautification. They have to do with young children. They're the kinds of supportive, nurturing, prettifying tasks and roles that have, historically, been associated with the woman's role in this particular culture.

Nancy Reagan's interest originally was in the Foster Grandparents' program. It's now in drug abuse. Rosalynn Carter, who was interested in hard policy, still made it a point to become involved with mental health. Lady Bird Johnson was very involved with highway beautification. Jacqueline Kennedy redid the White House. These tend very much to be the same kinds of roles, women's roles more than anything else. It's not just a question of volunteerism.

On the issue of the relationship with and the support of their husbands, the nature of that support really differs enormously from First Lady to First Lady, and the nature of that support depends on nothing as much as their relationship to the President.

First Ladies in general have not been strikingly successful in lobbying for their causes. I have to be careful when I say that because, in many ways, they have drawn attention to their causes, and attention breeds success in a way that could never happen unless they had focused their attention on these particular issues.

By the same token, when people look back on First Ladies, they don't particularly associate them with their causes any longer. Perhaps Lady Bird Johnson and her beautification, conservation, and wildflowers is an exception to this. My prediction is that unless Nancy Reagan becomes much bolder in her approach to her very genuine interest in drug abuse, and does more for it, she will not finally be remembered for that. She will be remembered for her tie to her husband.

## DONNIE RADCLIFFE

*I*t was a serious effort on the part of her aides because they felt that it was necessary for her to have a significant and meaningful project. And I do believe that she has had a longstanding interest in drug abuse. But I think it

sort of grew without them realizing how successful it was going to become.

I don't believe she had her project well defined when she first came to the White House, because she was talking more about Foster Grandparents than she was about drug abuse. By the time a year had gone by, though, it became apparent that there had to be something more startling, more significant, for her to be involved in, and her aides realized that it could well be accomplished through a project on drug abuse.

## SHEILA TATE

$S$he sits there and those big eyes focus on a kid and the kid finds himself telling his whole life story to her, and they both sit there and cry, but when she leaves, the kid can say, "You know, here's someone so important, and she

Above: *At Little Rock, Arkansas, Central High School, September 1982.*

Right: *Celebrating the tenth anniversary of the Foster Grandparent program, October 1982.*

cares about me." And that's the feeling they got from that. That started building. She would go to prevention programs where she'd learn what the problems were that they were spotting in five-, six-, seven-year-old kids—basically self-esteem problems—and how they were dealing with it. And she was taking that camera, that media spotlight, and turning it around and focusing it on the issue, which is something she cared about.

That's another thing I can't emphasize enough. Her staff didn't want her involved in that issue. We dragged our feet. We looked for alternative programs. We said, "This is depressing. How will she make an impact?" So we came up with some upbeat things, things she could affiliate with, and she'd say, "This is nice, but drug abuse is important and I want to get involved in fighting it. When's our next meeting with so-and-so?"

She kept putting it back on course during that whole first year, and the smart thing was, she recognized that if she was going to spend four or eight years involved in an issue, it was going to be something she cared about.

## MARY JANE WICK

*S*he's always had a great concern about drug abuse in the world, not just in this country. And she feels

*She sits there and those big eyes focus on a kid and the kid finds himself telling his whole life story to her, and they both sit there and cry, but when she leaves, the kid can say, "You know, here's someone so important, and she cares about me."*

what's happened is a great tragedy. She has compassion for individuals, great compassion.

Imagine how terrible it is to be older in life and feel you still have something to give but you have nobody to give it to. And to be able to share that with somebody young and also have the young person be helped at the same time. It's really a wonderful program that started during the time her husband was governor of California.

She opened the eyes of people all over the world to the drug abuse of young people, because they are the future of our country and many lives have been ruined. I'm so proud of her. I really am.

## MICHAEL DEAVER

All I can tell you is that I can remember coming back here on an airplane with Nancy Reagan during the transition period and I said, "Have you ever thought about what you're going to do back here?" And she said, "Yeah, I've always wanted to get into the whole teenage drug-abuse problem." It was not a last-minute thing. It was not an attempt to simply recoup her popularity ratings. It was something she felt very strongly about and still feels very strongly about. All you have to do is go to one of those conferences.

## WILLIAM F. BUCKLEY

I think her drug effort is extremely important to anybody who had children who grew up during the sixties. I saw a picture of her in the New York *Daily News* centerfold and the caption was, "Mrs. Reagan Cheers Up Billy Buckley O'Reilly," a nephew of mine who was having trouble with drugs and was in a rehabilitation place, and she didn't even know we were related. I learned subsequently from him about the warmth of that exchange.

You have to remember that California in the sixties was the home of the drug culture. You have to remember also that her husband couldn't speak at any college in California for three or four years when he was governor because they wouldn't permit him on campus. So that the impact of the drug culture and all that it tends to suggest in terms of misbehavior and civil misbehavior means a great deal to her

as a result of the phenomenon of her having been First Lady of California during its most frenzied time.

I suppose that anything that any public figure does is subject to the charge of public relations to improve an image. You can say that about Florence Nightingale, that she was concerned about her image. You can say that the Queen of England has really no interest whatsoever in antiques but feels that she ought to every now and then go to an antique show. But the First Lady truly, deeply cares about this problem.

## BONITA GRANVILLE WRATHER

*A*mbition is a wonderful thing. I think that she has become ambitious for the good of our country.

*You can say that about Florence Nightingale, that she was concerned about her image.*

Certainly it took a great deal of ambition to plunge into that drug program, and a lot of ambition to get up in the morning and travel on planes and meet with psychologists and psychiatrists and meet with some of the young people who are on drugs and talk to them. It's been heartbreaking for her to see them. I think her ambition is channeled in a wonderful direction. It isn't an ego trip of any kind.

## JAMES ROSEBUSH

*E*very year, focusing on this international drug problem, Mrs. Reagan has sought to narrow her focus, and in some ways broaden her focus. It seemed very obvious because of all the requests she was getting from First Ladies around the world to share information and knowledge about what she'd done on drug abuse, to expand it on an international level.

It wasn't that suddenly I arrived on the scene, or that 1982 was here and this was a brand-new plan. She made a commitment to drug abuse a couple of years before that. In fact, during that first year she was educating herself about drugs. Now, hindsight would say that should have been promoted more. People should have known that she was meeting with those people and so forth. But the fact was she was doing the right thing first, and that was becoming knowledgeable about the issue. The plan was in place all along for her to be able to get out, get to treatment centers, and so forth, and she'd been to some treatment centers before.

We gave her the options. We came up with places for her to visit—treatment centers. Our role was basically to say, "Let us be your eyes and ears. You want to travel around the country? You want to talk to kids? You want to find out about their problems? Our role as a staff is to help you do that." And that's what we did. And that's where we put sixty thousand miles on the plane.

Watch Nancy Reagan in action. You can't fabricate love. You can't fabricate concern, at least to the degree that she's shown it. This isn't something you can manufacture. You can't instantly have the kind of rapport that she has with kids. She's like a magnet for kids. I've been there. I've watched it. I've seen kids of all ages drawn to her for some reason. I can't put my finger on it. There's a natural attraction there.

I think there are a lot of concrete results. Thousands of parents' groups have formed coalitions to do something: shut down head shops; get legislation enacted; meet together to boost each other's morale and get their kids out of trouble.

Just through the television show "The Chemical People," which she hosted and which was the largest grass-roots effort ever undertaken on television, local communities are organized now to fight drugs. Making a national priority out of this issue is what a First Lady of the United States can really do. I think she's accomplishing that.

She's got a commitment in her blood now. She sees the dimensions of the problem, and she wants to solve it. She always asks wherever she goes, "What else can I do?" I think you're always going to see her working hard on it.

*Watch Nancy Reagan in action. You can't fabricate love. You can't fabricate concern, at least to the degree that she's shown it. This isn't something you can manufacture. You can't instantly have the kind of rapport that she has with kids.*

# 8

# The First Lady and Politics

## NANCY REAGAN

eople say I'm a very savvy politician? Well, that's flattering. True? I don't know. Maybe that gets more into the realm of people, of having a feel for people.

My husband projects tremendous trust in the American people, really tremendous. After how many years in politics, my husband is still underestimated by whomever he might be running against, underestimated by the press. But the people have felt that he was sincere and honest and that there was an integrity there. And they responded to that.

I was upset after the first presidential debate in 1984. I thought they'd gone about it all wrong, and they had. They overloaded him. He knows all those things. They don't have to overload him.

I suggested some changes. The second one was better, wasn't it?

Did Al Haig leave because of me? No, no, no, no, no, no, no, no, oh, no. Is it true that after the 1984 election I wanted to clear the dead wood out of the Cabinet? I thought that, in reading history, I'd always been given to understand that at the end of your first term that was a logical time, if you

*People say I'm a very savvy politician? Well, that's flattering.*

wanted to make changes, to do it. Yes, I did think that. And what happened? Not much.

Did I want the presidency more than he did? I read that. Not true. I thought I married an actor. He was asked to run for office soon after we got married, and turned it down. He was asked by the Democrats when he was still a Democrat. And when the governorship came along, I went along with it. But that wasn't something I had carved out for our future.

## ED ROLLINS

*T*he President is very pragmatic, and he has very good political instincts and very good people instincts. But I think there is no question that Nancy can step back and probably take a little better view of it than he can, being involved in the day-to-day aspect of it.

*Did I want the presidency more than he did? I read that. Not true. I thought I married an actor.*

Right: *Bowling with oranges aboard Air Force One during the 1984 campaign. This pastime became a favorite during takeoffs as Willie Nelson's "On the Road Again" played over the PA system.*

She called me from time to time in the course of the campaign and raised concerns about particular things that might be happening around the country. She has a very good network out there, and, most of the time, when she calls me, she's got very valid points.

She was very concerned in the California campaign during the 1984 election that the people out there were probably not being as effective as they could have been and that Mondale was making a very heavy effort in the state, and she wanted to make sure that we were alert to it. We were, but certainly, when she made her call, I went out and rechecked everything again and made a few changes.

She's a darned good, savvy politician. I certainly would value her judgment. I think both she and the President don't like to think of themselves as politicians. He is someone who sort of shies away if you say, "Politically, Mr. President, you need to do this." But I think he has superb people instincts, and she does, too. She happens to be a much better politician with this particular candidate because she's lived with him and knows his strengths and weaknesses so well. But nevertheless, I would certainly always want her on my team.

I don't believe she tries to get involved in the appointment process, but I think that she certainly wants to measure people who work for her husband and wants to make sure that their effort is a total effort.

The two of them prefer not talking ahead of the actual election. I remember when Richard Wirthlin and I were briefing the two of them coming across country on the Sunday before the election. It was very obvious that the President, according to the public opinion polls and all private polls, was going to win a tremendous victory. They wouldn't believe it. They just wanted to wait until election day. That's always been their style. They didn't live as close to the polls or the numbers and what was going on around the country as some of us in the day-to-day aspect of the campaign did.

She was not involved in the details of the campaign. She was the person who sat there day in and day out with the President and, basically, had to react one way or the other to what was going on and to the charges that were being made by the other side. She was not calling people in the campaign getting daily or weekly updates. We tried to talk to her every couple of weeks to let her know what was happening, and kept her pretty confident that we were doing what was right.

I think she felt that it was very, very important, as we started a second term, to have the very best we could get, and there were some people who had not worked out as effectively as was hoped when we started this administration. I think her concerns were concerns shared by many people who advised the President. She wasn't in the forefront. I think she had conversations with the head of personnel here in the White House, and with Jim Baker, and with Stu Spencer, about what it was that we needed in the second term.

All of us feel this is the big leagues and you ought to be able to play in this league, and if you can't, it's just like the National Football League or NBC News. If you can't cut it, you ought to be replaced.

Left: *Normandy, 1984.*

Right: *A private swearing-in ceremony in January 1984, the day before the public event.*

*She was the person who sat there day in and day out with the President and, basically, had to react one way or the other to what was going on and to the charges that were being made by the other side.*

The First Lady felt that the staff had probably over-briefed the President for that first campaign debate. There was no question he wasn't as relaxed. I believe it was just the fact that he hadn't been in the arena in a long time. Mondale had fifty-three debates in the course of the primary season before our debate. It'd been four years since the President had had any. I think she was very concerned that he perform well the second time.

Walking off the stage, he was the first one to make the comment that his performance in the first debate wasn't a typical Reagan performance. She felt it was imperative that maybe the staff get out of the way and the President just get ready for the second debate the way he was most comfortable.

Right: *At an American military cemetery in France.*

Far right: *A serenade during lunch at Maison des Tranneurs, Strasbourg, France, May 1985.*

## LYN NOFZIGER

*I* think she's played a very important role in her husband's political career. She's a very smart woman. She is very politically astute. I sometimes think that if there weren't a Nancy Reagan, there wouldn't be a President Reagan or maybe even a Governor Ronald Reagan.

She has certainly been a motivating force in his life. This doesn't mean she controls him, or tells him what to do, or that he's under her influence. But it does mean that they discuss together the direction in which he goes.

They're a very close couple. They talk things over. But you must remember that back in the middle and early sixties, a lot of people came to Reagan and said, Run for governor, run for the Senate, one thing or another, and he always said no. He was happier doing what he was doing. I think that if Nancy had said, "Ronnie, don't run for governor. I don't want you to; this is the good life," that he would probably have made the decision not to. The fact that she was

*I sometimes think that if there weren't a Nancy Reagan, there wouldn't be a President Reagan or maybe even a Governor Ronald Reagan.*

*She's an adviser, a confidante. She is unafraid to tell him what she thinks he ought to hear or what she thinks he ought to do.*

very supportive and has been all along has been an integral part of his campaigns, an integral part of his ambitions, if you will. It's made all the difference in the world.

She's an adviser, a confidante. She is unafraid to tell him what she thinks he ought to hear or what she thinks he ought to do. Once again, it doesn't mean that he does it. It's not a formal role and it's not a role that sees her active in the White House as a policy person or as somebody who views herself as part of the White House staff or the Cabinet. I think Ronald Reagan has been very lucky to have Nancy there.

## STUART SPENCER

*S*he looks for loyalty to the President and to his programs. I can't say she looks for anything else particularly. She commands loyalty, and she feels that anybody working for the President should be a loyal person.

She looks for talent that fills spots. When I came back into the Reagan operation in 1980, it was at her behest, basically, and the President's. They were having problems, politically, and she has always viewed me as a good politician, either when I was with them or against them, which I was in 1976. So they wanted me to come back because they felt they needed my political skills.

She usually works through other people. She informs them of what her thinking is. Her great strength is the fact that she's a conveyor of information to staff that the President would not convey to them. The President's not the type of person who's going to come down in the morning and say, "Stu, you really screwed up." He just won't do that. But he might say to Nancy, "Boy, you know, I think Stu really screwed up on that one the other day." She'd call me up and say, "Spencer, you really screwed up!" You get the message. You could go for two or three weeks with Ronald Reagan and not know he's mad at you.

We include her in a lot of the decision making in the political process when we're in a campaign. If we're having a discussion with the President and we're, maybe, losing the discussion, and we think it's a strong enough point that should be made, we might enlist her help if we can. She doesn't always go with us. Many times, she thinks we're wrong.

She's a very good politician. She has the skills and the instincts of a politician and she's tactically very, very, very strong. He's probably stronger strategically, but tactically, to get things done, she's very good.

He has the big picture. He understands the strategy of how he wants to get from here to there, and maybe some things that can happen. But she understands better how you get from here to there.

She is a conservative. They're like-minded ideologically, but she is always concerned about the fact that you can't govern unless you have public approval, and she recognizes that fact. And to keep your approval ratings up, your perceptions have to be up. She wants him to be able to govern, to accomplish the things that he wants to accomplish, and he's only going to be able to do that if his approval ratings are good.

She didn't make life tough for me after I supported Gerald Ford over her husband in 1976, but I got several messages in the back channels so that I knew very well where she stood. I don't think I saw her from that period until 1980. I don't recall even talking to her in that period of time. I was the leper.

In 1980, I didn't want to get involved in an effort like that, with all the problems that were potentially there, unless I knew I had the support of the principals. I think my biggest single problem after the '76 campaign was more

*She has the skills and the instincts of a politician and she's tactically very, very, very strong. He's probably stronger strategically, but tactically, to get things done, she's very good.*

*I don't think he'd have become President of the United States without Nancy Reagan. Because of her drive, her support system, she saw him through the good and the bad.*

with her than it was with him, because he's more forgiving, in a lot of ways, than she is. So I wanted to make sure that that base was covered. I knew her feelings were stronger than his about what had happened in 1976.

I think he would have probably gotten elected governor in 1966 with anybody else as his wife. He was a hot property in California. He was a new face. They were looking for a change and his timing was excellent. But I don't think he'd have become President of the United States without Nancy Reagan. Because of her drive, her support system, she saw him through the good and the bad. He spent a lot of time on the road between 1974 and 1976, looking for the nomination. And then it was grasped away from him, so to speak, by circumstances. And then they came back, in 1980, and she was there the whole time. Tremendous support system.

Ronald Reagan maintains that the office seeks the man, and that's the major disagreement that he and I have. If you want to be President, you go get it. I mean, if you really look at Ronald Reagan's record from 1966 on, he was running for the presidency in 1968. He went out and he went after it. He wanted it badly.

In the last campaign, the President was at the top, Jimmy Baker was next, and then we all fed into Jimmy and he fed it into the President. As we were developing our ideas and concepts, we'd feed it back to Nancy if we felt there was a problem. Some parts of the political process, like precinct organization, phone banks, coalition building, etc., etc., she understands. Other things she doesn't understand, but she knows how her husband likes to operate. She knows how he looks best, and how he's feeling, and you just have got to keep her plugged in.

I wouldn't emphasize the toughness. I think she can be tough, but she's a very sweet person, too, and a very warm person. I wouldn't want to suggest that she's just a tough woman. There are a lot tougher women in this process than she is.

If you ask the question, "Are you generally favorably or unfavorably impressed with the President?", you'll probably get numbers in the high seventies. When we use something called a feeling thermometer, which is a very different rating, the President's ratings have been quite close to Nancy's.

I think the extent to which Nancy Reagan brings a dimension of concern about important issues to the forefront, issues that are widely supported by a large number of Americans, to that extent, it does help the President. There's no doubt in my mind that Nancy Reagan is a strong political asset to the President of the United States.

I don't think there was a lot of concern inside the White House that Nancy was becoming a political problem. But I do recall having conversations with some of the political pros outside of the White House at that time. They said Nancy Reagan could never be a major help to the presidency, and therefore she should simply keep a low profile. If that counsel had been followed, I think it would have been a disaster both for her and for the President. I'm of course personally pleased that she pursued a very different and much more active route.

As I said earlier, Nancy has very good political instincts. In the latter part of '83 and the first part of '84, Nancy reviewed with me at length how she viewed the potential Democratic contenders, and gave me as good and as clear and as helpful an analysis of Mondale and Glenn and Hart as any of the so-called political pros. In fact, her judgments and her instincts in some ways were even more closely attuned to what the realities turned out to be than some of those who are paid for their political judgment.

In October of '83, she felt that Glenn simply would not get the nomination, and she saw the Hart phenomenon of that January before the New Hampshire primary, when he really did emerge. She tagged Hart as someone who could give Mondale a run for his money. She felt that Mondale would likely be the opponent. She believed his biggest vulnerability was his tendency, his penchant to attack, and

*Her judgments and her instincts in some ways were even more closely attuned to what the realities turned out to be than some of those who are paid for their political judgment.*

*She's able to size up political motivations rather quickly. She's been involved, though very much in the background, in politics for eighteen, nineteen years, and she's learned a great deal in that period.*

do it in a way that would alienate rather than gain support. She was right on target on that particular judgment.

She's an excellent pol, especially when it involves making judgments about people's assets and liabilities. She's able to size up political motivations rather quickly. She's been involved, though very much in the background, in politics for eighteen, nineteen years, and she's learned a great deal in that period.

Nancy Reagan is a realist and she's also very willing to make some tough decisions on personnel. I think I realized that for the first time when there was a change in the 1980 campaign staff. Nancy Reagan felt very strongly that a change should be made. She's willing to make and suggest some tough decisions.

I talk to her quite frequently. In a number of those discussions, we review the things that I know she's interested in. She's interested in the President's job rating, the mood of the country. She's also interested in how her rating is doing.

She has a good deal of sensitivity about communicating messages. The President is identified as the Great Communicator. Well, Nancy Reagan has an awfully good sense as to what kinds of messages can be communicated clearly and which cannot. I think she recognizes correctly the importance of leadership, not only as an end in itself, but the importance of having someone who is viewed as a strong leader to open up other options that wouldn't be there to a person who is viewed as less consistent and less strong. She views politics, again correctly, as a personalized activity—that is, people judging people and whether or not they trust an individual, whether or not they believe that individual is sincere. These are things she ranks relatively high.

Whether or not to run for a second term was an open question for Nancy until quite late. I think she was finally persuaded by November or December of 1983. She was still very open on whether the President should run and how she felt about that until sixty days before he announced. From what I know, they sat down, reviewed it together, looked at the pluses and the minuses, the challenges that would come from running for a second term. By November, by December, Nancy had pretty well decided that, given the President's feelings, she would support his running for a second term.

## PRESIDENT REAGAN

*N*either one of us ever really set out to do what we find ourselves doing. When the group came, in

1965, after the '64 election when I had supported the candidacy of Barry Goldwater, I had always thought that my contribution could be that, being a performer and thus well known and maybe able to attract an audience, I could support people and causes I believed in. Never did I ever think that I would want to hold public office. And this group came after the party had been so torn apart in the dissension of that campaign. California was split and they said that maybe we could have a hand in bringing it together. They kept emphasizing that I could win.

Our first reaction was, you know, "Don't talk foolishness. Go find a candidate and I'll be very happy to do everything I can to help him. But, no, that's not for us. That's not our way of life."

Well, they kept on and on until we couldn't sleep. It seemed to be such a total change of our entire life that finally I said, "What if they're right?" and "What if this is something and we wouldn't be able to live with ourselves if we keep on saying no?"

So the deal I made then, with perfect confidence that it would not result in my running for office, was, "All right, you set it up so that I can accept all the speaking engagements here in California, not just political, chambers of commerce, things of that kind, and let me do it for the next six months. I'll come back and tell you before the six months is over, whether you're right, that I should be a candidate, or whether there's somebody else. And I'll continue doing what I've been doing in the past."

And they did that, and I did my best out there. People would come up after a speech and say, "You ought to do this," and I'd say, "No," and I'd start talking to someone

*Neither one of us really set out to do what we find ourselves doing.*

*Sometime after I'd become governor, and we were sitting in the living room, all of a sudden it came to both of us that what we were doing made everything else we'd ever done seem dull as dishwater—that was the expression she used.*

else. I finally came home one night and said, "They're right. I think I do have the best chance of winning."

We almost decided between ourselves that, when I finally gave in and said yes, I would do it with the idea in mind that it was only for the election, that when the election was over I could go back to doing what I was doing.

Sometime after I'd become governor, and we were sitting in the living room, all of a sudden it came to both of us that what we were doing made everything else we'd ever done seem dull as dishwater—that was the expression she used. And it was true. I had never anticipated sacrificing something I loved doing for something that was really going to be a chore. But instead of just talking about the problems from the outside, to actually deal with them and to have a hand in solving them—well, one man who was a governor back when I was a performer had said to me about his job that sometimes he went home feeling ten feet tall. We both felt that way about it.

# 9

# *The Assassination Attempt*

## NANCY REAGAN

*I* remember everything about it, everything. I'd gone out to lunch and for some reason, which I still don't understand—we'd almost finished lunch—I said, "I think I'd better get back to the White House," and I got up and left.

I came home and I was upstairs and a Secret Service man came up and said, "I'd like to see you." I went down the hall and he said, "There's been a shooting but your husband's all right." Well, I was halfway down the elevator and I said, "I want to. . ." and he said, "No, it's all right. He's all right. They'll be bringing him back here. He's all right." I said, "I want to go," and we started out. We got there and they were waiting for me in the hospital to tell me that he had been hit.

I can remember the sound in the hospital. I can remember the confusion, the voices, the people running back and forth, the police telling people to get away.

I can remember being put into a little room—I think maybe three people could've gotten into it—where I still

*I can remember the sound in the hospital. I can remember the confusion, the voices, the people running back and forth, the police telling people to get away.*

would be if Paul Laxalt hadn't come along and said, "Don't you think we could put Mrs. Reagan in another room?" I remember wanting to see my husband and being told I couldn't, and then finally seeing him and the wonderful humor and strength that came through when he looked up and said, "Honey, I forgot to duck." I remember everything, going into the operating room, the smells, everything.

I don't think that's something that goes away. You both have your own separate traumas. I'm sure he has his, but I have mine.

You learn to live with that. You have to. You know that everything's being done that can possibly be done, but, you know, everything's gotten so much worse all over the world.

I was pretty beaten down. Then, my father was ill. I lost weight. I knew all the rumors going around saying I was ill, and I couldn't tell them really why I was losing weight.

*I don't think that's something that goes away. You both have your own separate traumas. I'm sure he has his, but I have mine.*

As I look back on it, I think I was in a state of shock much longer than I realized. My husband, I think, understood it more than I did. He was the one who suggested that I go to England for the Prince of Wales' wedding because he felt that if I got away and went to a royal wedding—and when am I going to get a royal wedding again?—it would be good for me. But it was his idea.

It's something that you don't forget. I thought, maybe, it would fade a little, but it doesn't. Every time he leaves the house, particularly to go on a trip, I think my heart stops till he gets back.

I really didn't worry before. You know that that's a possibility and so on, but you never think it's going to happen to you, and when it does, it's a shock that stays with you. If the President worries about it, he doesn't tell me. Some things are just too painful to talk about, aren't they? Life is always peaks and valleys, and that was certainly a valley.

Did it give me more a sense of mortality? Oh yes. You rearrange your priorities very quickly.

When anyone asks me about the security and Secret Service and doesn't it bother me and so on, I say not at all. I'm very happy to have them. If it weren't for them, I wouldn't have a husband.

## PRESIDENT REAGAN

*I* think it took her longer to heal than it did me, and I can understand that. I was confident that I was going to be all right and all, but I'm sure it would be harder for me to have to stand by and see someone else and have the worry that goes with it.

Just picture the difference. All right, it's happened to me and I'm there and I know, and I'm going to the hospital and so forth, but the shock to someone at home on what's a normal, routine day, and someone walking in and saying what has happened—that's got to be a lot worse than it is for the person it happened to.

## WILLIAM F. BUCKLEY

*T*he assassination attempt was so tough on her that I think she sincerely regretted that he'd run for President. And it was during that period when at least I had

*Every time he leaves the house, particularly to go on a trip, I think my heart stops till he gets back.*

the impression that she was very cool at the prospect of his running again. Gradually, that fear was overcome. And then, of course, when he decided that he wanted to run again, that became dominant in her own thinking.

She didn't want to risk her husband's life unnecessarily. And she thought that perhaps that was being done. That was during the height of her apprehension that, well, he came very close to dying, as we all know. She knew it all along. Her reaction to it was totally protective. Why should he run that risk?

## MICHAEL DEAVER

*I*t was a tough time. We had a lot of conversations both in person and on the phone trying to keep her up. But she's a strong-willed lady and I think that whole experience, as it did all of us, strengthened her.

It was tough. Her life is Ronald Reagan, and she came very close to losing him. And then she had her father's death a little bit later. But this could have been the big loss of her life. I can remember myself—and her feelings would have been a hundredfold what mine were—going home and saying to my wife after ten days, after seeing the President ten days after he was shot, I said, "Carolyn, I'll never be the same." If I felt that way, my God, what did Nancy Reagan feel? I knew she couldn't sleep. I knew she wasn't eating. I talked to the doctors about it and I said, "You really have got to get in there because she doesn't look well." And her friends were all coming around, bringing her candy and cookies and trying to give her encouragement and get her to fatten up a little bit.

## MAUREEN REAGAN

*W*e had lived for years with the knowledge that something like that could happen, but you're never prepared for it. She was not prepared for it. Nor was she prepared for the fact that—despite his humor and his climbing out of it—he was very seriously injured, much more seriously than anybody knew at that time. I was there a week after the assassination attempt, and I can tell you it was pretty bad. She sat there, in that hospital, all day long. Every two hours, they would go in and they would physically pound on his back to try to get the lungs to release this fluid that was building up. You could hear this. It was like somebody slapping a side of beef. She just sat there and would say, "That's your father they're doing that to." She sat there all day long with that, day after day after day. That has to take a toll on anybody, much more than I think any of *us* realized, much less anybody in the public.

*It was tough. Her life is Ronald Reagan, and she came very close to losing him. And then she had her father's death a little bit later.*

# 10

# Family and Friends

## Nancy and Her Children

### NANCY REAGAN

*I* think I've been a good mother. Many times discipline is left to the mother because fathers are busy. Certainly, we had a father who was busy. So Mother ended up being the disciplinarian, which is not always a happy role. Our children were growing up in the sixties, which was a terrible time to try to raise children, for children and for parents both.

I believed in discipline. I did not believe in being permissive or that, if they wanted to color the walls with crayons, it was okay. But I hope they always knew that I was there if there was a serious problem.

Ron didn't plan on getting married the way he did. He and Doria got to the marriage bureau and there was all this press there. They didn't expect that. So they thought, rather

*The family gathers for the 1985 inaugural. Front row: Bess Reagan, Neil Reagan, Colleen Reagan holding daughter Ashley Marie, the President and grandson Cameron, Doria Reagan, Anne Davis, Patricia Davis. Back row: Maureen Reagan, Dennis Revell, Michael Reagan, Patti Davis, Ron Reagan, Jr., Geoffrey Davis, Richard Davis.*

than having to go through this twice, we'll do it. And as soon as they did it, they called us to tell us and explain to us. It's a little misleading, the way it's been reported.

Patti was in Paris and they got the engagement ring. As soon as they got back here, they called, and we had a very nice wedding and they're very happy.

As far as Michael is concerned, every family has periods of misunderstandings or difficulties or whatever you want to call them. They solve them. The main thing is that you try to solve them, and hopefully you do. But you're lucky if you have a private life and you can do it privately rather than in the papers.

I don't believe in talking about family in public.

*But you're lucky if you have a private life and you can do it privately rather than in the papers.*

Above: *Christmas Day, 1985.*

Right: *With Ron, Jr.*

Far right: *At the 1984 Republican National Convention with grandson Cameron.*

All I said about Michael was the one sentence about trying to settle a problem and I never said anything more. Again, that was blown up into such a big thing. Every family has their problems at one time or another. No family can go through life without problems from time to time. We're all human beings.

I certainly would have tried to stop it if one of my children had gotten involved in drugs. I wouldn't have sat back and said, "Well, this is just a phase they're going through, and they'll come out of it, and somebody else will take care of it." I never would have done that. I might have failed, but at least I would have tried. I don't think some parents try enough.

I think they [the children] probably smoked marijuana at one time or another but they didn't smoke it and smoke it and smoke it. I understand it. It's like having the first cigarette. But it's a good deal more harmful, very harmful.

Do I worry about what the loss of privacy will do to my

children? Yes. Although they're older now and it should be a little bit better for them. It's very difficult for the children of people in public life, certainly this kind of public life. It's very hard.

## DR. BARBARA KELLERMAN

*I* think one of the interesting things to look at when you're looking at a First Lady is the really enormous increase in importance of the President's family since about 1960. There are very powerful, systemic reasons for that, why the President's family—not just the First Lady but parents of the President, children of the President, siblings of the President, all of them—can play very powerful political roles. It's really interesting to look at the entire family dynamic.

*It's very difficult for the children of people in public life, certainly this kind of public life. It's very hard.*

It's also very interesting to come to understand the reasons for this increased role of the presidential family, and those reasons are really very simple and very obvious, for example, the impact of television. Suddenly, families are known quantities in a way they could never have been before. The decline of the political party, the decline of the importance of the party in the presidential process, means that presidents don't have a whole cadre of party cronies to rely on any longer. So who do they rely on? Friends, and family.

The increased importance and frequency of the primaries, the demands of the primary system, mean that the President has to blanket the country with his presence. Very often, he draws on his family members to do some of the campaigning for him. Their wives, to be sure, but also children and siblings and parents.

You only have to look at the Carter campaign in '76 and even '75 to understand how Carter depended on his family to become known in this country. He was an unknown quantity in '75. By '76, he was well known—and a good part, the lion's share, of the credit for that goes to the various members of his family.

Finally, there's the changing culture. When Harry Truman was President, which is not all that long ago, he considered it unseemly for women to participate in political life, and told his wife and daughter so. The changes in culture, not only political culture but social culture, make it positively appropriate and desirable that women of all ages should play political roles.

*Finally, there's the changing culture.
When Harry Truman was President,
which is not all that long ago, he
considered it unseemly for women to
participate in political life, and told his
wife and daughter so. The changes in
culture, not only political culture but
social culture, make it positively
appropriate and desirable that women of
all ages should play political roles.*

The Reagan family, despite their early efforts to give a contrary impression, are in fact a very atypical family, and the main way in which they're atypical is the lack of closeness, or the apparent lack of closeness by conventional standards, between the parents and the children.

Some of the reasons for this are obvious. Two of the four children are from another marriage. But it's interesting to note that even the two children that Nancy and Ronald Reagan share, that they've had together, are relatively distant from the White House. I don't mean to suggest they're estranged from the White House. But I think families in general tend to stay in closer touch than the Reagans do with their own children.

Certainly the past White House patterns have had grown children far more active in and supportive of their parents' political lives than the two offspring of Nancy and Ronald Reagan.

## DOUG WICK

*I* think she is a very good mother. She's in the intolerable situation of having every yawn or wink examined under a microscope. I've certainly had my ups and downs with my family, but if I had to read about them every other day, I think it would be pretty disconcerting.

It has to be very painful to have people criticize you as a mother. I think her kids are crazy about her, though they've had their ups and downs, like any American family.

## C.Z. WICK

*I* think what you have is a very caring, supportive individual. When Ron decided to go into dance, the tabloids were reporting "Parents Upset Over Irresponsible Decision," or something like that. In fact, what happened was that they were very supportive and very interested in his career desire and, basically, they only said, "Well, we hope you love this, and we know you'll be as good at it as you can be." That's pretty much continued to be the case.

All the kids call when they need some solid advice, and I think that family holidays are important to the family, too. A sense of humor is another one of the characteristics of her relationship with all of her kids.

*Ron and his mother are good friends. They enjoy each other's company. The friendship has gone way beyond mother and son and the attendant duties of being a son or being a mom.*

I think that all the kids in the Reagan family are very independent. They're individuals, and any time you have a roomful of adults, all strong individuals, like any family, there are going to be differences of opinion.

Ron and his mother are good friends. They enjoy each other's company. The friendship has gone way beyond mother and son and the attendant duties of being a son or being a mom. They're both well-read, bright individuals, who have a terrific sense of humor and enjoy being with each other. They have fun together.

She is a very private person. An average family who are not in the public eye, a family that has strong individuals all with different opinions, if that family has differences or friction, they're able to work those things out in the privacy of their home. Nancy Reagan is somebody who would like to be able to work out any family problem or enjoy a family triumph or pleasure in the privacy of her home.

I think her unwillingness to share every detail of any family disagreement is probably what got the stories started.

If she and the kids and the President had been able to work out the normal family disagreements without cameras stuck in the window and microphones in their faces, it would have been a lot easier.

## MICHAEL REAGAN

In Hollywood, she was probably the best of mothers because she literally gave up her career when she married Dad and had children. Most actors and actresses in

*With the Michael Reagan family, January 1985.*

Hollywood, because of their egos or whatever reason, maintain that life. She gave it up. She said, "I'm not acting any more. I'm giving it up. I'm staying home with the kids." And so she gave up a career to be with Ronald Reagan.

We all live in a fishbowl. The bottom line is everybody loves each other, but you still are going to have family squabbles. I'm sure everybody does. First Family squabbles are like having arguments in a base drum—they reverberate. You can't have them behind closed doors.

Take Thanksgiving dinner. The press is always asking those questions, "Where is he?" because so much of the public out there expect you to always be at your dad's or your mom's for dinner. The only question for them is, "Do you always eat at home?" People ask, "Why don't you live at the White House?" I'm forty years old. I like to live at my own house. I think people misinterpret things in their own minds: "If my dad were President, I'd be there every night." Well, Dad's President. Dad's Dad to me. He's not just President of the United States.

Everybody in this family, Maureen, myself, Patti, Ronnie, will walk a plank for Ronald Reagan and Nancy. We'll walk off a bridge if that's what it takes, working to get him elected. Giving up time out of our lives, which we felt free to do.

But we're all individualistic enough to say, "But we've got our own lives." We've got to do that, too. Sometimes we're questioned about what we're doing—and people really hate to be questioned all the time. "Why are you doing this?" "Why are you doing that?" When Dad became President, none of us lived at home. And I think this is the first President in many years to have none of his kids living at the White House at the start of his term. So everybody searched this out, trying to find out what we were doing, why we were in business. People say "Gee whiz, Ronald Reagan must have a lot of money, why do you work?" So, if you work, they say, "Gee whiz, don't they like you?" But if you don't work, you're a bum. So what can you do?

Dad and I have talked about his not seeing my daughter until she was nineteen months old. Ever since Dad was shot, he has had such a feeling of his presence endangering other people. We were talking about it the other day. He asked me if I went to church. He said, "Gee, I wish I could go to church every Sunday." Because he worries about being in the presence of people. He comes and he visits Ashley and visits Cameron and spends the kind time with them he would like to everyday. Then their faces get all over television and everybody knows what they look like. And he wants to keep them in the background as much as possible. He doesn't want to endanger them.

*Everybody in this family, Maureen, myself, Patti, Ronnie, will walk a plank for Ronald Reagan and Nancy.*

He calls them on the phone and talks to Cameron. Ashley's now starting to talk a little bit on the phone. From one side, you really understand it, and from the other, being a father, being a parent, you say, "Gee, I wish he could spend some time." Once we're able to sit down and take that three-thousand-mile gap and close it down to two chairs, talking to each other, we're able to solve that.

But basically he just feels he doesn't want to put them in the risky situation of having everybody knowing what they look like. It's pretty hard for the President of the United States to have a quiet time with his grandkids.

He'll be able to spend that time when he gets out of office. When he comes out here, he's got Patti, he's got Ron to see, he's got Maureen to see. There are a lot of people for him to see whenever he can get to California. So the times that he does see them, he wants to make quality time. He asked one time, "Should I come over to your house?" I said, "By the time your motorcade pulled up, they wouldn't want me to live there any more."

Is everything solved between Nancy and me? We all loved each other before we even walked into the meeting we had, and I think it's easy to solve any problem you might have if you walk into a meeting knowing that you love each other, and we all do. When we had some misunderstandings, we closed the gap of distance, and, once we did that, everything was really solved.

I lived with them for a couple of years and we were close. We used to go out to the ranch and things of that nature. She and Dad used to come up and visit me when I was a boy in school. For a time there, there wasn't Patti or Ronnie, just Maureen and me. There's a real closeness there. Then Patti and Ronnie were kids. Nancy had to give her time to them, which is the thing she should have been doing. There was a closeness. When I was a kid, I loved to have my back rubbed. I used to sit on her lap and would have her scratch my back.

I don't know any women or men who have been through a divorce who like to have their first spouses thrown up at them on a constant basis. *People* magazine showed how much money everybody made. They had Dad in one corner and Jane Wyman in the other. My mom doesn't like that any more than Nancy likes it or Dad likes it. And it gets thrown up because it'll sell an article or sell a newspaper or sell a magazine. And, jeez, that happened some thirty odd years ago. People don't like spouses brought up after a thirty-year

Left: *The First Lady, Michael, and Colleen.*

Below: *Thanksgiving at the ranch, 1985.*

*When we had some misunderstandings, we closed the gap of distance, and, once we did that, everything was really solved.*

period. You get a little bit tired of it. I don't think it's jealousy as much as you just get tired of always hearing it. It's ancient history.

# MAUREEN REAGAN

*I*t's very comforting that she's there. When I had the flu very badly, just before the inaugural, she was calling the doctor three times a day to be sure that I was going to be all right for the festivities. I was invited to go to a party on Sunday afternoon, and so, when they came back from Camp David, I said I was going out to this party. She said, "'Well, you can't go to that party. You're sick." I said, "No, no, no. I'm much better, really I am." And there I am, forty-four years old, standing in the hall of the White House, hollering, "Mom, all my friends are going to be there, I *have* to go!"

She called and told them I could only stay for an hour. I wanted to die, absolutely wanted to die. I said, "What are you, an Irish mother?" And she said, "Yeah, that's what I am, but you're going to get well."

I had two role models when I was growing up: Jane Wyman, who chose to be a motion-picture star; and Nancy Reagan, who chose to be a professional homemaker. They both made their choices. So when I got to be nineteen years old, I knew that I could be anything in the world I wanted to be, as long as I was willing to work at it, and I could make the choice of what I wanted to be because those women had done it.

I went to boarding school at the age of seven. I went because, at that time, living in the town in which we lived, my parents felt that it was much healthier for us to live in a stable environment than to be in the Hollywood scene.

I can't disagree with that looking back now, but as a child in boarding school, it's a little tough to understand because you think you're missing something and, of course, you are missing being at home. Okay. Because of that, all of my growing-up years were spent in a different kind of environment than they would have been if I had lived at home. So it's all part of what I know and who I am and how I feel about things. If you ask me, did I miss something, I missed a lot of things. I missed watching television when it was a little tiny screen because we didn't have it where I went to school. There were a lot of things that I missed, but am I unhappy about them? No. Would I do it differently? I don't know. I only know what I had and what I did, and I did the best I could.

*And there I am, forty-four years old, standing in the hall of the White House, hollering, "Mom, all my friends are going to be there, I have to go!"*

We're a family. I don't know how close other families are. I only know about us. For years, I lived in the East and I didn't see anybody. It wasn't because they didn't care about me or anything, but I wasn't here. If everybody got together here at Christmas and I wasn't there, it wasn't their fault. It wasn't my fault. It was just the way it was. I still felt that they were my family and I still felt that we were close.

## RON REAGAN

*S*he's been a very concerned mother. She's always taken an interest in her children, what they're doing, how they're doing, and wants a close relationship with them. She seems to understand me. You'll have to ask her other children how she's been with them.

I think she found it hard to understand rebellion in children. After all, she grew up in a broken home, and

*We're a family. I don't know how close other families are. I only know about us.*

wanted so much for her mother to come back from the road and playing the theaters and stuff, and wanted so much to have a father in the house. Well, we didn't come from a broken home. At least, I didn't, Patti didn't. So we didn't have that kind of burning desire for that sort of security and that kind of family life, like a lot of other kids. Most kids go through a phase where you say, "Chuck it, I'm going to go out and do whatever I want to do," and I think she found that hard to understand, a little hard to take. But I think she's gotten over it.

Was she mad at me about going off and getting married in New York? For a little while, I guess. She didn't have the wedding that she would have liked. She'd have loved to have flowers and white dresses and all that, and we just went down to the courthouse.

What happened was that we were going to go down there, and we got our license at the courthouse, and suddenly it occurred to us that in New York you have to wait between the license and the marriage in case you change your mind or something. We also realized that if we waited

She's been a very
concerned mother. She's
always taken an interest
in her children, what
they're doing, and wants
a close relationship
with them.

Left: *With Ron, Jr., and his wife, Doria.*

Right: *Nancy's stepfather, Dr. Loyal Davis, is inducted into the Royal College of Surgeons at the Irish Embassy, 1981.*

*If none of us children had ever come along, I'm sure they'd have been just fine together. But now that we're here, she needs us, too.*

the two days, the press'd be all over us, so we convinced the judge to waive the waiting period and just marry us on the spot.

If none of us children had ever come along, I'm sure they'd have been just fine together. But now that we're here, she needs us, too. She needs that larger family. She needed her parents as well, and still needs her mother. In some ways, she still does.

# *Nancy and Her Parents*

## NANCY REAGAN

My father was the first neurosurgeon in Chicago. He hated his name, Loyal, just hated it. Evidently his mother was reading a book or had seen the name Loyal, which she liked. But it was a name that was very fitting, one just right for him.

Left: *Nancy's mother and Dr. Davis, December 1982.*

Right: *A birthday party for Dr. Davis at Blair House shortly before the first inauguration.*

*He expected a lot of you, and that was a wonderful thing. You'd find yourself wanting to do more to please him, and that was why he was a good teacher.*

He was, as a young boy, very bright. He got out of college early. He got into medical school early and became a doctor at a very young age. He was brilliant, and his contributions to medicine are historic, really.

I think he helped set everything in place for me. He was a man of tremendous principle. If you told him the truth, he would do anything for you, anything. He was professor of surgery at Northwestern and his students would say what a tough teacher he was. And he was, fortunately. If I had somebody operating on my brain, I'd want them to be taught by a tough teacher. I'd want them to know what they're doing. But he was only tough for their own good, to make them really good.

He would leave little notes under my door. Sometimes he'd leave me little poems, and I remember one time we had a disagreement about something. I don't remember what it was about. He left me a darling little note under the door the next morning.

He was a disciplinarian. He expected a lot of you, and that was a wonderful thing. You'd find yourself wanting to do more to please him, and that was why he was a good teacher. He would make you rise to heights you didn't know you could reach. But he was very fair. Always fair. If he said no, then he would always explain why he said no. It would be hard for his students to understand, but underneath all of that strictness, he was a soft touch.

Was it hard for him to transmit emotions? Not with me. Not with my mother.

A lot of my values and a lot of my beliefs, much of what I think is important in life, I got from him. Integrity. The value of integrity. The value of doing the best job you can no matter what the situation is, no matter what is presented to you, no matter where life takes you. The principle of always

*A lot of my values and a lot of my beliefs, much of what I think is important in life, I got from him.*

*He was just a marvelous man, and one of the hardest times I had that first year in the White House was his being sick.*

being fair, always being honest, always being truthful. He was just a marvelous man, and one of the hardest times I had that first year in the White House was his being sick.

I miss him very much, very much. Even now. I remember a letter from a couple whose child was sick and he drove to their home to take care of the little girl. She had a tumor. He saved her life and then, a little bit later, she became sick again. He went back and operated on her again. After the first time—and they sent me a photostat copy of this—he drew them a diagram of what was wrong, and then he said to them, "I hope you'll understand that I have to send you a bill. I don't want to send you a bill." They didn't have much money. "But I have other people to consider here." And I think he sent them a bill for a hundred dollars—something like that. I think he operated on her three times eventually, and he always kept in touch with them.

He was dying, and the first year in Washington was not a great year and this was one of the major reasons why it

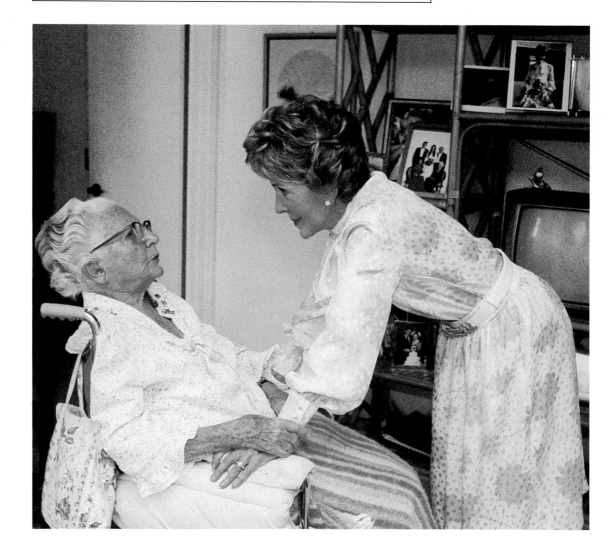

wasn't a great year. He was dying and I would talk to him on the phone every night. But then, when it got to the end, I went to Phoenix and took him to the hospital. And my mother, we told my mother he was going to have some tests. And I stayed there and he died around nine P.M. I've never seen anybody die before and certainly never anybody I loved. After that I was afraid that my mother would hear it on television or the radio, and I didn't want that to happen. So I had to leave the hospital and go to my mother and tell her that he was gone.

I speak to her every night. From the White House or wherever.

The time passes so quickly, and your time with your parents passes so quickly. When you get right down to it, they're the ones who are going to put their hands in the fire for you. They're the ones who are going to stand up for you.

*The time passes so quickly, and your time with your parents passes so quickly.*

## NANCY REYNOLDS

*I* think one of the lowest points I have ever seen Nancy Reagan was when the President was shot. That's in a class by itself. Nothing can describe that. But she was very strong during that period, too. And very upbeat trying to nurture others who were so upset.

It was when her father died that I saw her at the lowest period I've ever known. I think she felt the loss more keenly than she ever believed she would, even though he had been quite ill. She spent those last days with him. She was down in the dumps, as any of us would be. She certainly wasn't eating very well. I think the President was deeply concerned about her. And then we all were when he was. But, of course, time does heal, and her mother is still needing her care and love. The loss certainly affected her greatly. He was a tremendous influence in her life. A wonderful man.

*Mrs. Davis is in a class by herself.*

Mrs. Davis is in a class by herself. What a privilege it's been for many of us to have known her. She is held in high regard and affection wherever we travel. It was astonishing how, wherever we would travel in the United States, some cab driver or some bellboy in a hotel or a manager in a motel would come up and say, "Mrs. Reagan, I knew your mother once. She was so kind to me." They always had a story about something Mrs. Davis had done for them. And we all knew that to be true, but it was astonishing the influence she had on people of all kinds, all over the United States.

## MARY JANE WICK

*I*t was very, very difficult. She was very close to her father. She loved him very much. It's very tough to say goodbye to somebody you love very much and who has been a very important part of your life. It was truly difficult for her. She'll have beautiful memories, but it was difficult. Very.

# Nancy's Friends

## MICHAEL DEAVER

*S*he calls me whenever she wants to. It depends on what's going on that day. You're talking about a relationship that's now nineteen years old, and Nancy Reagan's a best friend to me. There isn't anything we haven't talked about over the years. I look at Nancy and me as a team. We are friends. I've never looked at it in terms of people listening to me because I'm Nancy's buddy. I've never thought about it that way. I think she's very supportive and very happy with the new team. She's very fond of Don Regan, and thinks he's doing a good job. They have a very good relationship, the Regans and the Reagans.

I was at the White House during the rocky start, and I was here during the good years, too. She doesn't know a lot of this new team, so I'm sure, being the worrier that she is, she probably thinks about that. But I don't intend just to walk away from the White House, either. I've got a lot in-

*It was when her father died that I saw her at the lowest period I've ever known.*

*The President's been Santa, and Ron's
been Santa. We've all had our turn.
It was Mrs. R's turn this year. Ron was
not with us. She was on the phone
with him while we were putting the
pillow on and the crazy suit and all the
rest, and it was great. She was one
of the better Santas on record, I'd say.*

vested here with these two people, and I'm going to be helping them.

## SHEILA TATE

*I* liked working for her. She's the first woman I ever worked for, though I don't think that dawned on me until several years into it. She's very detail-oriented, and because I am also detail-oriented, I found it easy and enjoyable to work for her because she knew what she wanted. You learn to anticipate her needs and what she wants. I found it a very productive place to work.

To some degree, she is a worrier. She admits that. But she doesn't worry unnecessarily. If she's been provided with all the information about an event, she's not going to worry about it. But if there are holes in it and she sees there are holes, then she'll worry. She'll call you and say, "What's going on at this event? Who's on the dais? Who will I be sitting with? Are their remarks available in advance? When do I get there? When do I leave?" She wants to know that sort of thing, and I think that's smart. I found that that was a plus. Now, if you weren't used to that, maybe it would be hard on you. But I think her staff enjoyed that about her.

I always enjoyed being in her company. She had unique observations. She was funny. You felt a little protective of her. She has that vulnerable quality, and yet you know she's a very secure, well-defined person in her own mind with regard to what she does and how she does it. And yet you get the feeling that she's this tiny little person who needs to be protected. She is complicated, and that makes her very interesting.

## NANCY REYNOLDS

*I* think she expects the same of you that she expects of herself, her husband, and anyone who's around her. That's not an unreasonable demand, in my book. She always is willing to listen if you give her good reasons why a suggestion must be made. One of the joys of working for both the Reagans was that they never equated disagreement with disloyalty. So we often disagreed on many issues and I would have to back it up every time I would say, "Well, I think you should be doing this," or "I think we ought to

*Left: "One of the better Santas" with C. Z. and Doug Wick.*

think about this." I would have to back it up with some awfully good arguments. Usually, her commonsense won.

## C.Z. WICK

*I* guess I've known her twenty-five or twenty-six years and I know her really well. As someone of a different generation, I can provide, maybe, a look at her that the average person who reads or sees a report on the news doesn't get to know about.

We were family friends dating back to early elementary school days, and she's really been a personal friend. You always have a special relationship with a friend of the family. It's been a close, one-on-one relationship. It's been that way since I was a little kid. It wasn't so much adult-to-kid as it was friend-to-friend, and continues that way.

She's a terrific person to bounce things off of, someone who's going to put your best interests first and not try to steer you in a direction that doesn't feel right.

I remember when I decided not to practice law, after law school. I called up and I said, "I want to sound you out on something because I'm feeling this." And when I told her my reasoning for getting into another business, she said, "I've been expecting this call," not, "Boy, it'd be a lot safer if you'd join a firm and kept that suit on." She understood from knowing me that I was interested in other things. It's nice to have somebody who knows you well, who can give you an objective response, a real helpful way of looking at things.

My family has a tradition. Christmas Eve is a big deal for us, and there's been a Santa Claus ever since I was born. At first, to convince you that there was one, and later, when we ran out of young kids, because it was still something we wanted to do, and the tradition involves having some close friend play Santa each time.

Well, when my family moved to Washington and I ended up commuting to Christmas, we'd have Christmas Eve at our house and then we'd go to the White House and have Christmas dinner with the Reagans. The President's been Santa, and Ron's been Santa. We've all had our turn. It was Mrs. R's turn this year. Ron was not with us. She was on the phone with him while we were putting the pillow on and the crazy suit and all the rest, and it was great. She was one of the better Santas on record, I'd say.

Being Santa entails coming into the living room on the cue of "Jingle Bells"—a very original piece of dramatic

*She's a terrific person to bounce things off of, someone who's going to put your best interests first and not try to steer you in a direction that doesn't feel right.*

work—and sitting in a big high chair and having everyone in the room sit on your knee and tell you why they should get whatever they want for Christmas. Humorous rejoinders from Santa are part of the tradition, and she has a way of coming up with them. Everyone was very careful when sitting on her knee. After all, it's not like when I sat on her knee twenty years ago. We had a great time.

As close a friend as she is, I wouldn't feel right calling her Nancy. You find a fond way of referring to someone without crossing that line, and it has nothing to do with something I've heard from her—just my own perception. Because she and my mother are so close, I could always rely, if I was out of town or not around or something, on calling her if my folks weren't home and finding out what was going on, because they're in close enough touch. If someone did well in school, or there was some family business that I didn't know about, I could always trust her to do it. So "Secret Agent 007" was sort of an ongoing joke between all of us. And looking for that special kind of nickname that

*As close a friend as she is, I wouldn't feel right calling her Nancy. You find a fond way of referring to someone without crossing that line.*

characterized a special relationship, "Double O Seven" sort of stuck, and that's pretty much what I call her.

My folks were looking for a house-warming gift when the Reagans moved to the White House. There's plenty of silver there and plenty of the things you would get a newly-wed couple, and somehow the thought of Camp David and all those great trails they have up there came to mind, so my folks got them a bicycle built for two, figuring that a spin around the property up there would be great. They had it delivered to the White House, and Ron and I decided when we were visiting to take her out and give her a spin. She put on her jeans and we went out on the driveway by the South Lawn and took a few turns.

One of the earliest memories I have of her as a friend was when I was seven years old and playing the genie in some school play—that's a big deal when you're seven. It would probably still be a big deal if I were still doing it. She was the first person backstage to say, "Boy, was that great." You really knew she was listening and watching. She was always there. When we were living in Los Angeles and she

was in Sacramento, there was always that call: "Heard about so-and-so, and boy, was that great." She's someone who's there for you.

The Reagans were in Sacramento and I was delivering something to the house. I didn't know if she was going to be there. I hadn't seen her in a while and, in those days, had hair down to my shoulders and a beard and walked in in a work shirt or something. Sure enough, she was there. I said, "Jeez, I wish I'd cleaned up a little bit," and it was like old times. I think there were a couple of aides around and it was as if I'd seen her yesterday. There was no hesitation about my appearance.

She's always asking me when I'm going to bring some nice girl over to meet her. I've told her I wasn't ready yet, and that if it happens or when it happens, my parents have a used brick patio that would need a little cleaning up before the wedding. She'll say, "I'll scrub it for you, and I won't forget." So the joke is that I have this old pair of knee pants at home and she will say, when I tell her about someone I've met, "Is it time to take the knee pants out yet?"

# DOUG WICK

She's a very good friend. She's one of those people who values her friends and makes an effort to keep and to build the friendships. She's someone who, if you're going through a troubling period, you know you're going to get a phone call from, and she'll try to be constructive. And she's consistent. No matter what's going on in Washington, she still makes an effort to stay in touch.

She's very good with advice. I was going through a kind of romantic crisis and the Reagans were over at my parents' house for Christmas. I was getting a little obsessive about this problem I had with my girlfriend, and I spent two or three hours talking with her in a corner. You never would have known I was slowing things down. It turned out I'd kept dinner an hour late, but she's someone who listens and responds, and then calls you two weeks later and tells you you'd better get off your duff.

She's one of the great lunch dates in America, and I think if everyone in America got to have lunch with her, she'd be one of the most popular woman in the country. She listens, she's smart, she's got a good sense of humor. I have a lot of show-business friends who have gone to Washington and, no matter what their politics were, if they happened to spend time with her, they always came away with great

*She's one of the great lunch dates in America, and I think if everyone in America got to have lunch with her, she'd be one of the most popular women in the country.*

*I think she's certainly at her best one-on-one because she relates that way. She relates directly to you, person to person.*

reports because they found her engaging and smart, and whatever preconceptions they had were always changed.

I think she's certainly at her best one-on-one because she relates that way. She relates directly to you, person to person. In groups, she's not someone who thrives on being the center of attention.

## MARY JANE WICK

The first time we met, our children were going to nursery school together. It was a small school and the parents would get involved. As a matter of fact, she and her cousin manned the hot dog booth during the school fairs.

We had our interests, children and families, friends, being involved in the community together. She has a really marvelous sense of humor. She's very funny.

We were involved with the Colleagues together. The Col-

leagues started out as a home for unwed mothers. Then it later became a home for abused children and affiliated with the Children's Hospital in Los Angeles. We have a large sale each year in Santa Monica—used clothing, all kinds of used carpeting, furniture, antiques, furs. People come from all over the country to buy or sell.

Nancy has many friends all over the country. She's a wonderful friend. They were all involved in different activities in Los Angeles. Most of the people who are friends of both of ours are people in community activities. Most of her friends were very supportive during her husband's campaigns.

She's a friend of mine. I see all the positive things she did when she was the wife of the governor of California and when she was his wife before he was governor. She's still a very good person who's done so much for so many people and so many causes. She cares.

## BONITA GRANVILLE WRATHER

*I* first met Mrs. Reagan about thirty years ago, and I met Ronald Reagan when I walked on the set of a film at Warner Brothers called *Angels Wash Their Faces*, and he was the male lead and Ann Sheridan was the female lead. I was one of the Dead-End kids.

Our circle of California friends formed over a period of years. I think we all came together in the early sixties when we felt California needed a leader. A lot of the gentlemen, Earl Jorgenson, Dale Wilson, William French Smith, Justin Dart, Holmes Tuttle, and my husband, tried to talk Ronald Reagan into running for governor. And after that, the friendship was cemented. We enjoyed being together. We enjoyed doing the same things. And, of course, we were all of the same political persuasion.

Nancy Reagan is probably one of the most loyal friends a person could have. She has deep sympathy and empathy, and she's very loyal to her old friends as well as her new friends. I think Nancy is a very special human being.

*Nancy Reagan is probably one of the most loyal friends a person could have.*

# 11

# The Years to Come

## The Ranch

## PRESIDENT REAGAN

The house was built in 1872. It was adobe, plaster-covered, kind of a not too pretty brown. There was a screened porch, with green plastic sheets around the bottom, and an aluminum corrugated ceiling that went across just above your head. We had a contractor come in. We wanted it enclosed and stuccoed so it would match the plaster. This is the only thing that we didn't do, that we had professional help for.

We'd get a fire going and we'd lean tiles against the screen to soften them up. They'd get very rubbery and we'd grab those and put them on the floor—feed them in while we put fresh ones up there to soften up. This was easier than the rest of the house because, built a hundred years ago, I guess they didn't have good square measures and things. There wasn't a square corner in the rest of the house. So when it came to tiling, we had to figure out a way to lay the bulk of the tile and then, around the edge, cut the tile to fit the different widths that were left.

This ranch really casts a spell. You sit out there, looking at that view. With our first ranch, Mulholland ran right through it about two hundred and fifty feet from the house. Here, you turn in the gate—it's just a road for a few ranches that are up here—and once you're inside, there's no sense of traffic or the outside world at all.

Nancy said the proper line one day. I've used it, I've stolen it from her a million times since. "Presidents don't get vacations. You just get a change of scenery." Now I spend much of the morning before we ride on the phone making calls, and there is the usual paperwork that comes in several times a day. The job goes with you. You're not taking time off. You're not really escaping anything.

But the main thing is, we aren't here that often. Think back on other presidents: Ike and Augusta; President Nixon with the Western White House plus the place in Key Biscayne, Florida; John F. Kennedy with Hyannisport and the farm in Virginia.

*This ranch really casts a spell.*

*A joint Christmas present, a 1985 Ford Ranger pick-up truck for the ranch.*

*The White House has magnificent quarters and we're very well treated there, but you are kind of a bird in a gilded cage, and they don't open the door very often to let the bird out.*

The White House has magnificent quarters and we're very well treated there, but you are kind of a bird in a gilded cage, and they don't open the door very often to let the bird out.

I think I'm very conscientious. We both think about responsibilities and what must be done. But I also know what this ranch means. There is a line in the scriptures that describes it: "Look to the hills from whence cometh my strength."

## NANCY REAGAN

I think it's important for people to get away from Washington, for a President to get away from Washington. It can become very insular, and you think that Washington is everything—that it's the be all and end all. It's not. It's important to be away and get a whole different feel and perspective and hear different voices.

When you think of other presidents, some of it is that they've gone for vacations to places that were very close.

Half the time people didn't even know they were gone. But for us, our home is farther away.

Was I nervous about bringing the Queen of England here for lunch? I was, until she got here. That whole trip, nothing happened the way it was supposed to, starting with the weather. There's something about things not going according to schedule that makes everybody kind of relaxed and makes it more spontaneous and you feel more cozy somehow. She was dying to get up here. She got in the truck and she crossed the streams and all of that.

You can get outside here and walk, ride, you know, all those nice things. I've read those stories about my being bored here. Not true, not true. But how many times can you keep saying, "It's not true"? Pretty soon you say, "Well, if they're going to say it, they're going to say it."

I know it's not true. I know I love to come here. I know it's very peaceful.

*You can get outside here and walk, ride, you know, all those nice things.*

# The Judgment of History

## JAMES ROSEBUSH

*I think she hopes to be remembered as a First Lady who cared about people and was supportive of her husband.*

She's seen that she can have an impact. I think she hopes to be remembered as a First Lady who cared about people and was supportive of her husband.

The only indication we have now is what the polls tell us at this time, but I think she'll rank very high, because of the substantive issue that she's gotten into. It's not an easy issue. It's a very emotional one.

That's just the beginning. You'll see Nancy Reagan traveling more abroad, accepting invitations from those First Ladies she's already visited with here, and perhaps some other countries, too. You may see another conference, another summit. I think this is the beginning of her leadership on an international level. I've observed her at very close hand. I've seen those feelings and commitments deepen.

One of the first things I was impressed with about Nancy Reagan was when she said to me, "I'm not going to become something that I'm not." Over and over again, she'd tell me that.

I think it's for history to tell, but my opinion would be that she has left an important mark on history.

## MICHAEL DEAVER

*I* think she understands better now than she did at the beginning that she is in a position for the first time in her life to be more than just Mrs. Ronald Reagan, that she can do something with her life independently that can bring about a change for the good, whether that's in the drug-abuse program or whether it's the way she deals with foreign visitors. I think Nancy Reagan understands that she herself can be a force for good.

I see that in her. I see that she understands that the first role in her life is always going to be Ronald Reagan's Nancy. She also sees that she can take some time and do something else where she can make a contribution, too.

## WILLIAM F. BUCKLEY

*E*leanor Roosevelt wanted to be an activist. She wanted to be thought of almost as Mrs. Wilson was thought of. But I think the mark that Nancy Reagan wants to leave is that of having—and I pay her no dishonor by saying this—been an exemplary First Lady. Are you doing everything one expects of a First Lady? And if you say that's making a mark, then I will say, well, anybody who wants to approach the paradigm, wants to make a mark.

## BILL BLASS

*I*t will be difficult to judge whether or not she will twenty years hence have the same impact as Mrs. Onassis. Perhaps it's because when Mrs. Onassis, as Mrs. Kennedy, arrived at the White House, she was still young. She was not a trend setter, either, for that matter, but she did

*I think the mark that Nancy Reagan wants to leave is that of having been an exemplary First Lady.*

*I never really thought about how I'd like to be remembered as First Lady until somebody asked me the other day...I guess the best answer I can give is that I cared, that I tried to make things better.*

have an impact simply because she was young and it was the first time in many generations, many decades, that a First Lady had style.

## RICHARD DAVIS

She has made her mark in several ways. I think the contemporary mark she'll leave could be the drug-abuse program. The lasting mark would be how she is perceived in the years to come as a wife, a dear friend, adviser, confidante of her husband. I think that's probably the most important thing to her.

## NANCY REAGAN

I never really thought about how I'd like to be remembered as First Lady until somebody asked me the other day. I never have thought about it, but I guess the best answer I can give is that I cared, that I tried to make things better.

# Contributors to the White Paper

*Richard Allen*  Washington lobbyist and consultant Richard Allen was President Reagan's national security advisor during his first term.

*Letitia Baldridge*  Author Letitia Baldridge is an internationally recognized authority on etiquette and manners. She advised Nancy Reagan and was Jacqueline Kennedy's social secretary.

*Bill Blass*  Fashion designer Bill Blass has long been a friend to Nancy Reagan.

*William F. Buckley*  William F. Buckley is a syndicated newspaper columnist, publisher of the *National Review*, moderator of television's "Firing Line," author of numerous nonfiction books and novels, and one of the nation's leading conservative thinkers and lecturers. He and his wife, New York society leader Pat Buckley, are longtime friends of the Reagans.

*Michael Deaver*  California publicist Michael Deaver was another Reagan family friend who followed the president to Washington where he served as one of Reagan's top three White House assistants before resigning to become a capital lobbyist. He is considered one of Nancy Reagan's closest friends.

*Betty Friedan*  Author and lecturer Betty Friedan has been one of the principal leaders of the feminist movement.

*Dr. Barbara Kellerman*  Dr. Barbara Kellerman, a full professor in the Institute for Leadership Studies at Fairleigh Dickinson University in New Jersey, is an authority on First Ladies.

*Lyn Nofziger*  Family retainer Lyn Nofziger served Ronald Reagan as a political advisor during his years as a governor and presidential candidate. He was a presidential assistant in charge of White House political affairs and is now a private political consultant.

*Donnie Radcliffe*  A former California journalist who also worked for the *Washington Star*, Donnie Radcliffe is social editor of the *Washington Post* and writes its "Washington Ways" column. She has covered Nancy Reagan and the East Wing of the White House for much of her career.

*Michael Reagan*  Michael Reagan is the adopted son of Ronald Reagan and his first wife, actress Jane Wyman. A California businessman who has also raced motorboats and acted, Reagan and his father and stepmother have had strained relations in the past, but a reconciliation was effected in November 1984.

*Maureen Reagan*  Maureen Reagan is the daughter of Ronald Reagan and his first wife, Jane Wyman. She has involved herself in a number of careers, and turned to politics in 1982, running unsuccessfully for the U.S. Senate from California. Despite earlier strained relations, she and her stepmother have become good friends and Maureen has undertaken White House projects for her father.

*Nancy Reagan*   As an actress, political wife, First Lady, and champion of causes, Mrs. Ronald Reagan has been in public life for four decades. She told her personal story in her own words in interviews with Chris Wallace and NBC News, and those interviews were incorporated into the text of *First Lady*.

*President Reagan*   President Reagan was pleased to be interviewed for the NBC special on his wife, Nancy Davis Reagan.

*Ron Reagan*   The Reagans' youngest child, son Ron left Yale University to take up a career as a ballet dancer and performed with professional companies. After his father became president, he left the field of dance to persue a career in journalism, covering politically related events for *Playboy* magazine and other publications.

*Nancy Reynolds*   A reporter in California, Nancy Reynolds joined the Reagan staff in Sacramento and became a Reagan family friend. She played a key role in the transition from the Carter to the Reagan administration and has subsequently worked as a leading Washington lobbyist and public relations consultant.

*Ed Rollin*   Another Reagan political advisor, Ed Rollin succeeded Lyn Nofziger as the chief political affairs assistant in the White House and has since become a private consultant.

*James Rosebush*   James Rosebush worked as an oil company executive, Commerce Department official, and special assistant to the president before becoming First Lady Nancy Reagan's chief of staff in Reagan's first term. He has since returned to the private sector.

*Stuart Spencer*   Veteran Republican strategist Stuart Spencer served Ronald Reagan in a number of political campaigns, though he also worked for Gerald Ford in 1976. He is now a private political consultant.

*Sheila Tate*   A longtime public relations executive in Denver and elsewhere, Sheila Tate was Nancy Reagan's first press secretary.

*Doug Wick*   Doug Wick is a son of Mary Jane and Charles Wick. A producer for Columbia Pictures, he lives in Los Angeles.

*C.Z. Wick*   C.Z. Wick is the oldest son of Mary Jane and Charles Wick. He works for Prime-Time Program Development Department for ABC, Los Angeles, where he is the Director of Dramatic Series Development.

*Mary Jane Wick*   A close friend of Nancy Reagan, Mary Jane Wick is the mother of Doug and C.Z. Wick. She met Nancy Reagan when C.Z. and Patti were in school together at John Thomas Dye School. Both mothers were involved in school activities and became fast friends.

*Richard Wirthlin*   Pollster Richard Wirthlin has advised President Reagan and other Republican public officials.

*Bonita Granville Wrather*   Former actress Bonita Granville married oilman, investor, and motion picture producer Jack Wrather in 1947, five years before the Reagans were wed. The two couples were California friends for years.